A-LEVEL YEAR 1 SOCIOLOGY FOR (

UNIT 1 (Socialisation, Culture & Ide

SOCIOLOGY PAPER 1 STUDY GUIDE
(with Youth Subcultures Option)

Published independently by Tinderspark Press
© Jonathan Rowe 2021, 2022
This edition © 2023
www.psychologywizard.net
www.philosophydungeon.weebly.com

This 2023 edition contains additional material on feminism and patterns & trends regarding youth deviance not found in the 2021 edition and updated advice on essay structure based on OCR input

Visit the **Sociology Robot** YouTube channel

The author is not affiliated with the OCR Exam Board and makes no claim to represent OCR's policies, standards or practices.

CONTENTS

ABOUT THIS BOOK

This book offers advice for teachers and students approaching OCR A-Level Sociology, **Paper 1 Section A (Socialisation, Culture & Identity)** and **Section B2 (Youth Subcultures**

Study Guides for **Papers 2** and **3** will follow.

Paper 1 Section A

This covers about a third of **Paper 1** in OCR Sociology. There are 3 questions worth 38 marks out of the 90 marks for the entire paper. It should take candidates 30-35 minutes to complete.

Paper 1 Section B (Option 2: Youth Subcultures)

This covers about two thirds of **Paper 1** in OCR Sociology. There are 3 questions worth 52 marks out of the 90 marks for the entire paper. It should take candidates 55-60 minutes to complete.

Perspectives

This Study Guide introduces candidates to 3 vitally important sociological Perspectives: **Functionalism**, **Marxism** and **Feminism**. In **Chapter 3**, **Interactionism** is introduced to make a fourth. Although other Perspectives like **Postmodernism** and the **New Right** are mentioned, they are properly introduced in the **Section 1B (Youth Subcultures)**.

Functionalism is, strictly speaking, an obsolete theory in Sociology, but its ideas remain very influential in politics and in the media. Even though students who move onto a degree-level study of Sociology at university will find that Functionalism barely features, it is presented here as a theoretical perspective that is both intellectually and morally equivalent to the 'conflict' perspectives of Marxism and Feminism. The aim is to help students evaluate sociological arguments from any point of view.

Studies

Sociological 'studies' (for A-Level purposes) are often papers published in academic journals, but are sometimes magazine articles, pamphlets produced by charities or activists or popular books.

Where texts are particularly famous or influential, I offer their names, but candidates are not expected to know the names of studies in the exam. All the studies referenced in this Study Guide are brought together at the end in a revision aid (p93 and p162).

SECTION A: SOCIALISATION, CULTURE & IDENTITY

What's this topic about?

This introduces you to the main theories in Sociology, in particular the concept of CULTURE (p7) and how it influences us. You will also learn about the SOCIALISATION (p30) process that prepares people with the skills and beliefs that are valued by their culture and the concept of IDENTITY (p62) which is how we perceive ourselves and others as part of a culture.

This should help you answer some important questions:

- What is our culture like: is it good? or bad? Is it even possible to judge whether cultures are good or bad?

- Is our culture changing? If so, in what direction is it going? Is that a good thing and, if we wanted to change it, how could we go about that?

- Are there some things that *aren't* down to culture: some things which are fixed and unchanging, which are the same everywhere and all the time? If so, what are they?

Capitalism

Probably the most common word you will come across in Sociology is '**Capitalism**' which describes the way society is structured in the UK as well as in Europe, America and many other countries.

Capitalism is the idea of **private ownership**: people own their own houses, other people rent from a landlord who owns the building. Some people own their own businesses and other people work for them as employees. Everything is owned by someone, nothing is automatically free or 'held in common.'

This focus on private ownerships leads to the other big focus in Capitalism: making a **profit**. Things are made and sold, not for what they are worth, but at a price which makes a profit for the owner. This pursuit of profit means that a boss will pay his workers as little as possible to increase the profits for himself.

Capitalism is often accused of being a system where a small number of people are obscenely rich and the vast majority must work hard in jobs they would never choose to do if they didn't have to earn a wage, which they need to buy the overpriced goods in the shops. Advertising makes people feel that money and buying things is all that matters – that your worth as a person is equivalent to what you can earn.

However, Capitalism is praised for being a system where people can get hold of the goods they need and where the pursuit of profit makes businesses efficient and hard-working. Capitalism has led to creativity and progress, new medicines, new technology, new fashions and new ideas.

By the end of this course, you should have your own ideas about the value of Capitalism.

CHAPTER ONE - CULTURE

Culture means the things that are shared by a society that mark it out as distinctive. You might think of Chinese people eating noodles with chopsticks as part of a 'Chinese culture' and British people drinking tea and eating fish & chips as being part of 'British culture.'

However, culture goes much deeper than just food and drink. In many states in the USA, ordinary people can own and carry guns and the USA has the highest rate of firearms-related deaths in the world: a study from 2016 showed that Americans were 10 times more likely to be killed by guns than people in similar countries. There are US states that still use the death penalty for serious crimes and do not allow same-sex marriages. This makes America very different from Britain, despite both being largely English-speaking democracies with a shared history. These are *cultural* differences.

Of course, not all Americans are gun-carrying fans of the death penalty and not all British people are tea-drinking supporters of same-sex marriage. Individual people can go against their surrounding culture and there might be entire areas or groups where parts of the wider culture don't apply: British Asians often have different attitudes to things than White British people; Hispanic Americans and New Yorkers often differ from other Americans in important ways.

Nonetheless, culture influences people in subtle and surprising ways.

Positive Views of Culture

Culture is viewed by some people in positive ways. It gives people a sense of belonging which might be important for mental health, low crime rates and success in work and education. It connects young people to their parents and grandparents, passing down wisdom from the past and preserving traditions. Culture is often linked with morality, since it gives people a powerful sense of what's right and what's wrong. Culture can be responsible for a 'sense of shame' that makes some behaviour unthinkable. Culture offers people a sort of plan or template for how to live their lives which can be very important in a confusing and ever-changing world.

This positive view of culture celebrates the symbols of cultural distinctiveness: flags, dress, local cooking, religion, native languages and accents, the expectation that you will marry within your culture and raise your children in that culture.

Negative Views of Culture

Culture isn't always positive. The sense of belonging can lead to pride and arrogance (termed *chauvinism*) and hostility towards outsiders who do not share your culture (termed *xenophobia*). Cultural traditions can be oppressive things; for example, expecting daughters to go without an education and stay at home to cook and care for the family. The 'sense of shame' from your culture can be crippling, especially if it stops you from being able to pursue your education, career or romantic relationships. The template for living that culture provides can be restrictive and it can blind people to other alternatives.

This negative view of culture is suspicious of cultural symbols: flag-waving is seen as **_jingoistic_** (a simple-minded view that your culture is best), dress codes can be oppressive, religion can cause conflict and bigotry, languages divide people and the pressure for people to 'stay in their lane' and raise families inside their culture only adds to these divisions.

Flag-burning is a powerful way of showing your rejection of aspects of a culture (photo: ManilaRyce)

Relativism, Chauvinism & Universalism

Chauvinism is the irrational view that your own culture is better than all the others. This can range from a group of music fans who think that their band is better than any other type of music to a nation that thinks their country is the best on earth.

Relativism is the opposite: the view that no culture is any better (or any worse) than any other culture. Relativists think that cultures are never right or wrong; they are only *different*.

Universalism is the view that some things are (or should be) shared by all cultures: a sort of stripped-down worldwide culture that everyone ought to belong to. The main example of this is Human Rights: supporters argued that these rights apply everywhere, even in places where the local culture disagrees. It's worth asking yourself if there really *is* a universal culture of rights, or if that is just the culture of Europeans and Americans (who came up with these rights) claiming to be superior to all the other cultures – a form of chauvinism.

When one culture starts imposing its way of life on others, this is termed **cultural imperialism**. This can happen because of a deliberate policy (such as forcing all children to be educated in the language of the dominant culture) but it often happens less deliberately, simply because the dominant culture makes its lifestyle and attitudes seem fashionable, exciting, modern or popular. The way Hollywood movies and Big Tech companies like Netflix spread American culture is sometimes viewed as cultural imperialism.

RESEARCH PROFILE: MEAD (1928, 1935)

Margaret Mead (1901-1978) is a pioneering researcher who visited Samoa and lived among the tribes of New Guinea in the 1920s. Samoa and New Guinea are islands in the Pacific and, in the early 20th century, the inhabitants had little contact with the outside world. Mead described her findings in *Coming of Age in Samoa* (1928) and *Sex and Temperament in Three Primitive Societies* (**1935**).

In Samoa, Mead studied 68 girls (aged 9-20) from three villages. She observed that they were allowed to experiment with sex – heterosexual and homosexual – in a way that would be considered shocking in America at the time, but that they grew into settled and fulfilled adults because of the absence of shame and stress.

In New Guinea, among the **Arapesh** people, both males and females were gentle and cooperative: stereotypically feminine according to American attitudes at the time.

Among the **Mundugumor** (now Biwat), both males and females were violent and aggressive – stereotypically masculine.

Among the **Tchambuli** (now Chambri), the woman were dominant and practical while the males were emotional and spent their time making themselves beautiful by arranging hair, jewellery and makeup – the *opposite* of the masculine and feminine stereotypes in America.

Mead's research shows that sexuality and masculine and feminine behaviour might not be based on biology. It is **socially constructed** behaviour that is learned through upbringing and traditions. **Social construction** is a very important concept in Sociology and is the main alternative to the view that culture has a biological basis in our physical needs.

However, Mead's research was criticised for putting her conclusions first then 'cherry picking' data to back it up. **Derek Freeman (1983)** travelled to Samoa in the 1950s and claimed Mead had exaggerated her rosy picture of the guilt-free Samoan adolescence and ignored sexual violence. He interviewed some of the Samoan girls and they denied their promiscuous behaviour, saying they had lied to Margaret Mead.

Deborah Gewertz (1981) studied the Chambri in 1974–1975 and found no evidence the unusual behaviour Mead describes.

However, it is possible that contact with the outside world made the Samoans and the Chambri change their behaviour after Mead studied them (for example, they had converted to Christianity). Moreover, Freeman was interviewing the Samoan girls now they were old women and perhaps felt embarrassed to admit their youthful behaviour.

*Mead's research and the debates surrounding it is very useful for you as a student. You can bring it into most essays about **culture** and **socialisation** and it's useful for discussions about **sexuality** and **gender identity** too. Lean into it: I've put it here first for a reason*

*Mead's research is described again in the introduction to **Section B (Youth Subculture)** on p99.*

PERSPECTIVES ON CULTURE

Perspectives are different ways of interpreting the social world. The three perspectives in this chapter are the main ones you will use for exploring **Socialisation, Culture & Identity** but another perspective (**Interactionism**) will be introduced later in **Chapter 3** (p67).

Perspectives are very broad viewpoints. Individual sociologists from the same perspectives might disagree with each other. Some sociologists straddle more than one perspective. I will take a neutral view on which perspective is "right" or "wrong" and focus instead on how they differ and the ways in which they criticise each other.

CONSENSUS PERSPECTIVE: FUNCTIONALISM

Let's start with the easiest and perhaps oldest perspective in Sociology: **Functionalism**. Functionalism is the view that **society has developed to reflect human beings' needs** and as our needs evolve, society will slowly change. **Functionalists** think that humans have biological needs which are fixed – they're big believers in inherited characteristics and biological sex, for example – so they don't think society can or should change too much. In fact, functionalists believe the best societies are those which most closely match and answer human needs. Since all humans have the same biological needs, this means there are going to be good and bad societies, with 'good' meaning 'best fitting our needs' and 'bad' meaning 'going against our needs.'

Most functionalists think Western-style democracies, with liberal and individualistic values and Capitalist economies, 'fit' human needs better than any other type of society that has been tried. They believe in the **'March of Progress'** with societies gradually improving (i.e. becoming more liberal and individualistic) so they reject the need for revolutionary change.

Culture is important for functionalists. It represents the wisdom of the past, the ideas that have 'stood the test of time.' Sharing a culture creates a **value consensus** – an agreed sense of how things should be done, what's important, the boundaries of acceptable behaviour and the things to be strived after. Participating in this value consensus gives our lives purpose and meaning; without it, humans suffer from **anomie** (a state of disconnection from society) which leads to depression, anxiety and destructive behaviour like crime, drug-taking and suicide.

Many Functionalists aren't personally religious, but they usually see value in religions like Christianity which support democracy, individualism and Capitalism. They also tend to support the nation state as the best way yet devised for humans to organise themselves politically. For most functionalists, 'culture' means the culture of your nation.

Functionalists usually view progress as a matter of trial-and-error. Lots of ideas and institutions have been tried throughout history but rejected – magic and witchcraft, divine kings, slavery – so they think the ideas that have survived must have value.

Functionalists claim institutions have a **manifest** (obvious) **function** – something they do that benefits society. However, they also propose that institutions can have a **latent** (hidden) **function** – benefiting society in non-obvious ways. For example, a latent function of religion might be to help people cope with stressful life events like births, marriages and bereavements (these milestones are sometimes called '**rites of passage'** and religions tend to bring communities together to acknowledge them). Even negative things like crime can have a latent function, like allowing people to vent their frustrations or experiment with new lifestyles.

Overall, functionalism tends to take society 'at face value' and views Western societies as the ideal, the sort that other societies should aim to be like. Functionalism finds value in religion and tradition, supports the family and the law and regards us all as being 'in it together' and sharing common values.

Historic Functionalist: Emile Durkheim (1858-1917)

The great French sociologist was (along with Karl Marx ad Max Weber) one of the three founding fathers of Sociology. **Durkheim** explored how modern societies struggled to maintain order and consensus during a time of great change. Durkheim argues a society needs: (1) **social solidarity**, which is a sense of being connected into a larger whole through common beliefs and commitments; this requires (2) **social integration**, which is a feeling of commitment to others often brought about by **collective ceremonies** (such as royal weddings and funerals in which we can "all share") and **collective identifications** (like the national flag).

Without social solidarity, people suffer from **anomie** (a state of disconnection from society) and cope with this by turning to crime, drugs or even committing suicide. Durkheim thought that modern Capitalist societies struggled to create social solidarity precisely because they were so big and confusing. Urban living (in big cities) is particularly difficult, leading to anomie and inner-city problems like rampant crime and misery.

You will meet Durkheim again when you study religion as **social control** (p58).

Contemporary Functionalist: Talcott Parsons (1902-1979)

Parsons was an American sociologist whose theories were popular in the 1950s – a time of exceptional stability and prosperity in America. In **The Social Structure of the Family** (1959), Parsons explores the functions of the family: to socialise children and stabilise adult personalities. He argues for strict **gender roles**, with men as the **instrumental leaders** (earning money, dealing with the world outside the family) and women as the **expressive leaders** (offering care and compassion inside the family).

You will come across Parsons again when looking at **socialisation by religion** (p37) and religion as a force for **social control** (p44).

CONFLICT PERSPECTIVE: MARXISM

Conflict is the opposite of consensus and this perspective rejects gradual evolution in society in favour of a sudden revolution. **Marxists** reject the idea that society reflects human biological needs – they're big believers instead in the influence of upbringing and work to shape our needs. Marxists believe that **society is shaped by conflict between groups with different economic interests**: a ruling class that holds the wealth and power in society and a working class that is much more numerous but poor and powerless. For them, there are good and bad societies, with 'good' meaning 'giving power to the working classes' and 'bad' meaning 'allowing the ruling classes to hold all the power.'

Most Marxists think Western-style democracies, with liberal and individualistic values and Capitalist economies, are particularly unfair and destructive. They believe in the need for revolutionary change to replace Capitalism with a fairer system.

For Marxists, culture does not represent the wisdom of the past, but rather the version of events preferred by the ruling classes. They reject the idea of value consensus because they think the rulers and the workers want very different things.

A key concept is **ideology** – a set of beliefs that people are brainwashed into holding that hides and justifies unfairness in society, persuading people to ignore or accept injustice as 'the way it has to be.'

Most Marxists view religions like Christianity as especially harmful, because they tend to support Capitalism and oppose revolutionary change.

Marxists also tend to oppose the nation state as an institution controlled by the ruling classes to divide the working classes.

Marxists usually view progress as inevitable. Older ideas and institutions get swept away by newer ones. Capitalism is a deeply flawed system but it is kept going by ideology and the power of the ruling classes. It will collapse eventually, but Marxists think we have a responsibility to end it sooner rather than later. Rather than focusing on the beneficial functions of traditional institutions, Marxists tend to focus on the harmful effects. For example, they often accuse religion of promoting war and intolerance.

Overall, Marxism tends to take a **critical view of society**, especially Western societies which are Capitalist. Marxism resists the influence of religion and tradition, criticises the family and the law and regards most of us as being manipulated and exploited by the wealthy ruling class.

Historic Marxist: Karl Marx (1818-1883)

Karl Marx gave his name to Marxism, which he explored in *The Communist Manifesto* (1848) and *Capital* (1883). Marx identified two parts of any society:

(1) **infrastructure** which underpins everything, including the **means of production** (land, factories, etc) and the **relations of production** (who are the owners and workers);

(2) **superstructure**, which includes all the **social institutions** (e.g. family, schools, religion, business).

For Marx, all the social institutions are shaped by the infrastructure, which means that whatever society *looks* like it really boils down to two groups:

(1) the **ruling class (Bourgeoisie)** who own the means of production and

(2) the **working class (Proletariat)** who *don't* own the means of production and have to sell their labour for money.

Marx argues that the Bourgeoisie exploit the Proletariat, keeping the wages low in order to make as much profit as possible. This causes class conflict. The Proletariat don't resist this because they of **false class consciousness**: they have been brainwashed into accepting this arrangement as normal and fair. However, Marx thought that one day the Proletariat would gain **class consciousness**, resulting in a revolution and the transformation to a Communist society.

It's sort of fashionable to use Marx's language of 'proletariat' and 'bourgeoisie' and part of the appeal of Sociology is showing off your vocabulary, so don't be afraid to use these terms in your writing.

Marx's ideas are examined again in respect to **alienation** in the workplace (p46)

Contemporary Marxist: Jock Young (1942-2013)

Jock Young investigated crime and the way it was reported in the UK news. He pioneered a new approach to criminology with *What's To Be Done About Law & Order?* (1984).

Young explored the idea of what he calls "**bulimic society**" obsessed with wealth and fashion: Capitalism creates crime because the poorest people are manipulated in desiring the trappings of wealth and success at any cost. Society is 'bulimic' because it encourages to be hungry for new consumer good which, as soon as we have them, we discard because we now want the latest, more fashionable version.

Young is a powerful critic of **Consumer Culture** (p21) as **alienating** and **exploitative**, forcing people to take on debt in pursuit of materialistic goods that they really don't need..

CONFLICT PERSPECTIVE: FEMINISM

Marxism is a conflict theory based around the idea of social class, but Feminists argue that **gender** is an equally significant source of conflict in society. Feminists reject the idea that society's gender roles reflect human biological needs – they're big believers in the influence of upbringing and experience to shape gender roles (the behaviour expected from males and females).

Feminists believe that **society is structured in favour of the interests of males**: although they make up half the population, women are subordinated to men, they are 'second class citizens' and are threatened with physical or sexual violence to keep them in line. For Feminists, there are good and bad societies, with 'good' meaning 'giving power to women' and 'bad' meaning 'allowing men to hold the power.' An arrangement where men hold power and status is called **patriarchy**.

Feminism has been through a number of 'waves' in the 20th and 21st centuries.

- **1st Wave Feminism:** In the 19th and early 20th century, women campaigned to be able to vote, inherit property, run businesses and go to university; the famous **'Suffragettes'** were from this time and succeeded in winning the vote for all women in the UK by 1928.

Suffragettes carrying arrows to proudly display prison status (photo: Julie Jordan Scott)

Research: the Suffragettes, the Vote for Women in different countries, the rights of women in the 19th century

- **2nd Wave Feminism:** In the 1960s and '70s and new generation of Feminists fought for equal pay, the right to contraception and abortion and freedom from harassment and damaging stereotypes. **Liberal Feminists** focused on improving laws and education to make society more equal but **Radical Feminists** argued for a completely new sort of society, with some claiming women could not live alongside men.

- **3rd & 4th Wave Feminism:** recent developments in Feminism will be considered in **Chapter 3** (p67)

Many Feminists think Western-style democracies, with liberal and individualistic values and Capitalist economies, are particularly unfair to women. They believe in the need for change to replace patriarchy with a fairer system, but they disagree on whether this change should be revolutionary or a gradual reform.

For Feminists, culture does not represent the wisdom of the past, but rather the version of events preferred by the patriarchy. They reject the idea of value consensus because they think males and the females want very different things. They often make use of the Marxist concept of **ideology** – a set of beliefs that hides and justifies the unfair treatment of women, persuading people to ignore or accept sexual discrimination as 'the way it has to be.'

Many feminists view religions like Christianity as especially harmful, because they tend to support patriarchy and interpret oppressive gender roles for women as ordained by God. They are alert to sexist **discourse** (messages and ideas) in the mass media – especially advertising, films and TV – and the way violence against women is excused or even celebrated in society.

Overall, Feminism tends to take a **critical view of society**, especially Western societies which are seen as strongly patriarchal. Feminism resists the influence of religion and tradition, criticises the family and the law and regards women as being exploited or threatened by males.

Historic Feminist: Mary Wollstonecraft (1759-1797)

This British author was the early pioneer of feminism with her book ***A Vindication of Rights of Women*** (**1792**) in which she argues that women are not naturally inferior to men (as was taught by Christianity at the time) and the only reason they achieved less than men was because they did not receive the same education. Wollstonecraft is considered a **'proto-feminist'** (a feminist before real feminism came along).

Contemporary Feminist: Ann Oakley (b. 1944)

This British sociologist and novelist wrote the article ***Conventional Families*** (**1982**), which explored how families raise boys and girls differently to **socialise** them into their gender roles, especially using **canalisation** (channeling children through the choice of clothes, activities and toys provided for them) and **manipulation** (the way parents speak to their children, the expectations they have and what they praise and punish them for).

You will learn more about Oakley when you study the family as an **agency of socialisation** (p39).

CULTURE: A TOOLKIT

Culture is sometimes used to mean the refined or sophisticated things in life: art, poetry, expensive fashion. However, for sociologists, culture means EVERYTHING that a group of people share: the common behaviour, beliefs and ideas of a society. In this sense, we can talk about *British* culture compared to *American* culture, because British people and Americans tend to have different ideas about how to live (like drinking tea, carrying guns or enjoying soccer).

Culture includes things like the food people eat (and how they eat it), the clothes they wear, religion, the history they know about, morality, the music and sport they enjoy, manners, the expectations they have of males and females, their views on children, the drugs they think are acceptable, the sexual behaviour they think is unacceptable.

Norms

Norms are the correct way of behaving, in line with cultural expectations. In British and American culture, strangers shake hands when they meet. In some Asian cultures, bowing is the norm.

People who go against norms are viewed as deviant. Deviant behaviour is sometimes seen as funny, but at other times it can confuse, shock or frighten people.

It's important to remember that norms are *behaviours*. You can go along with norms by doing the expected thing, even if you think it's silly or pointless. You don't have to *believe* in norms to fit in to society; you just have to act appropriately.

Norms change over time. The norms of male dress in the UK have changed from shirt-and-tie to jeans-and-T-shirt. Hats used to be the norm for men, but no longer. For women, norms of dress have changed to become more revealing, whereas it used to be very deviant for women to bare their legs or shoulders.

You will notice that out-of-date norms seem silly or fussy. That reveals something important about culture. While you are 'inside' a culture, its norms seem sensible, obvious, just common sense really. Cultural norms viewed from 'outside' often look quaint or ridiculous. Culture influences the way we interpret behaviour.

Values

Values are the correct way of thinking, in line with cultural expectations. British people often value fairness and tolerance. Americans often value success and patriotism.

People who reject cultural values are also seen as deviant: words like "wicked," "sinful" and "unnatural" are often used. Imagine if someone told you they didn't love their parents or didn't see anything wrong with stealing.

It's important to remember that values are *beliefs*. Since we can't read each other's minds, it's easy to conceal your own values and pretend to go along with what others think. However, great reformers and brilliant innovators usually have to defy the values of their culture about what's possible or how things ought to be done. For example, **Martin Luther King Jr** challenged the racist values of America in the 1960s.

You will notice that there are two sorts of people who defy the values of a culture: criminals and reformers/innovators. Often, only time will tell if someone treated as a criminal comes to be seen as a reformer/innovator. It depends whether the culture's values change to match them.

AO2 ILLUSTRATION: MULTICULTURALISM

The UK today – along with most European countries, the USA and many others – is a multicultural society. This means it is home to several distinct cultures, many of which are identified with ethnic groups who have arrived through immigration from the Caribbean, the Indian subcontinent, etc. Some of which have been in this country for a long time, such as the Jewish community or the Traveller/Roma community.

Multiculturalism is the view that this sort of society is desirable. Its opposite is a **homogenous society** – also known as a **monoculture**. How can a multicultural society maintain a set of consistent norms and values if it is home to many different cultures?

Leitkultur: This German word means 'guiding culture' or 'core culture' (**Bassam Tibi, 1998**). It is the idea that one culture in the multicultural grouping should be dominant. For example, the liberal-democratic culture that embraces secularism (religion purely a private matter) and equality. Immigrants must subscribe to the *leitkultur* to be allowed to settle.

Melting Pot: An idea from the USA, that immigrant cultures merge together into a blend. The largest immigrant groups will have the biggest effect on the blend, like the main ingredient in a soup. As more immigrants arrive – or as some groups grow through high birthrates and others shrink – the blend will be changed.

Salad Bowl: A more common idea in the UK, this is the idea of cultures keeping their distinctive way of life but living alongside each other. No cultural group is any more important than any other, although groups that experience oppression might need special help. This is a popular idea for **Intersectional** sociologists (p63).

Since 2002, immigrants have had to sit a *Life In The United Kingdom* test: 24 questions on British life, traditions and values. This is an idea taken from *Leitkultur*. However, the test has been criticised for being a "bad pub quiz" (**Radhika Sanghani, 2013**), asking questions that lifelong British nationals wouldn't know the answer to.

Research: take the *Life in the United Kingdom* test at https://lifeintheuktests.co.uk/life-in-the-uk-test/

TYPES OF CULTURE: HIGH CULTURE

High culture includes cultural products that have high status and are enjoyed by the elite. Cultural products include art, food, clothing, sports, language and lifestyle. High culture includes art like opera, food like caviar, clothing like top hats or ball gowns, sports like polo, refined language (such as saying "one" instead of he, she or I) and lifestyles involving riding horses, traveling by yacht, visiting the theatre and hosting dinner parties.

High culture is **exclusive**: it's not meant to be enjoyed by ordinary people. There are often barriers to entry, such as wines or restaurants using French titles, operas being in Italian or German, fine art requiring education to appreciate. Without these qualifications, people can find high culture baffling or boring.

High culture is **privileged**: it confers status on people who enjoy it or produce it. It marks you out as tasteful, sophisticated, intelligent and 'deep.' Knowing how to order from the wine list or what's going on in an opera helps a person fit in with the elite in society and distinguishes them from the *hoi polloi* (a Greek phrase meaning 'the common people').

An interesting example of high culture is the presence of Shakespeare in the British school curriculum. Shakespeare's plays are high culture and are not understood by most school children without a lot of education. Does high culture act as a barrier to children getting an education? Or does it offer an opportunity for children to aim higher, join the elite and acquire privileges?

AO2 ILLUSTRATION: SHAKESPEARE IN SCHOOLS

William Shakespeare (1564-1616) is considered the greatest writer in the English language and the world's greatest dramatist (he wrote 39 plays that are considered classics). Since 1993, Shakespeare has been a compulsory part of the National Curriculum in England, so GCSE students must study one entire Shakespeare play. Schools are not free to avoid teaching Shakespeare if they want to enter students for GCSE exams.

Many (perhaps most) students find Shakespeare's 16th century English difficult to understand and the Shakespeare component of the curriculum is nicknamed 'Shakesfear.'

Critics claim that compulsory Shakespeare only puts students off his plays and makes it harder for children from poor or immigrant backgrounds to pass GCSE English.

Some supporters use the Functionalist argument that High Culture like Shakespeare is objectively good and brings psychological and moral benefits – understanding Shakespeare makes you a better person.

Marxist critics like **Bourdieu** (see below) argue that there's nothing special about Shakespeare but that learning his work gives students **cultural capital**, allowing them access to power and prestige later on in life.

Although considered High Culture, the many film adaptations of Shakespeare's stories would be part of **Popular Culture** and **Global Culture** (because his stories have been adapted into Russian, Japanese and other settings). The 'Shakespeare Industry' selling books, documentaries and tourist souvenirs associated with Shakespeare, the Globe Theatre in London and his home in Stratford-upon-Avon is part of **Consumer Culture**.

RESEARCH PROFILE: BOURDIEU (1984)

Pierre Bourdieu (1930-2002) is an influential French thinker whose 1979 book *Distinction* was translated into English in 1984. Bourdieu based his theory on detailed mathematical analysis of two surveys of popular taste from the 1960s.

Bourdieu takes the Marxist idea that society is divided into classes based on economic capital (wealth) then makes this more complicated by arguing there is another type of capital: **cultural capital**.

Cultural capital is knowledge of **High Culture** and it is acquired through a privileged upbringing and education. Lack of cultural capital might keep a wealthy person out of the ruling class, because they don't have the cultural capital to 'fit in.' Possession of cultural capital might give a poor person access to upper-class society; for example, academics who understand art might mix with millionaires at an art exhibition.

Bourdieu claims each person has a **habitus** which is a collection of their personal habits (the way they speak, dress and think). Habitus reveals your cultural capital (or lack of it) and also makes it harder for some people to acquire cultural capital even if they have the money to buy art, visit theatres or get an education in the classics.

Many people assume that there is something objectively superior about high culture but Bourdieu is a **Marxist** and argues that there is nothing innately superior about cultural capital – as opposed to **functionalists**, who tend to think that high culture is objectively better than other types of culture. Instead, Bourdieu argues that the ruling class determine what counts as cultural capital specifically in order to exclude people from their privileges. For Bourdieu, the whole point about opera being sung in Italian is that it **excludes** people with a working class habitus from being able to understand it.

*Bourdieu's surveys will be looked at in more depth when you study methods as part of **2A: Research Methods & Researching Inequalities**.*

TYPES OF CULTURE: POPULAR CULTURE

Popular culture includes cultural products that have low status and are enjoyed by everyone. Popular culture includes art like hip hop or rock music, fast food like pizza, clothing like hoodies or T-shirts, sports like football, slang language (such as saying "hi" or "yo" to a friend) and lifestyles involving watching TV, playing video games, beach holidays and going to the pub.

- Popular culture is **inclusive**: it's meant to be enjoyed by ordinary people. There are few or no barriers to entry: anyone can dance to popular music, enjoy a big budget Hollywood movie or eat a burger.
- Popular culture is often **stigmatised**: instead of conferring status on people who enjoy it or produce it, it marks you out as tasteless, unsophisticated, uneducated or vulgar.

It's worth reflecting on whether popular culture *really is* inclusive. In many ways, it has rules that can be confusing to outsiders. Think about how your parents can be baffled by modern slang. Similarly, some popular culture is not stigmatised; think of films and TV dramas that are praised by critics for mixing high culture and low culture (such as *Game of Thrones* or *Bridgerton*).

AO2 ILLUSTRATION: HOLLYWOOD

Hollywood is a district in Los Angeles, California where movie companies like Warner Brothers built their headquarters and film studios back in the 1920s. The term 'Hollywood' has come to be shorthand for the mainstream American film industry that makes big budget mass-entertainment movies with internationally-famous stars that are watched all over the world. Hollywood is also termed 'the Dream Factory' because it helps people escape their everyday lives.

Other countries have their film industries. For example, French cinema is famous for being artistic, philosophical and high-quality rather than escapist fun – more like high culture than popular culture. Indian cinema is nicknamed 'Bollywood' (combining Bombay and Hollywood) because it imitates the optimistic, glamorous and escapist values of American Hollywood.

RESEARCH PROFILE: STOREY (2006)

John Storey is a Media Studies scholar whose book *Cultural Theory & Popular Culture* offers 6 definitions of popular culture: (1) culture that is **widely-liked** (no stigma implied); (2) the **opposite of High Culture** (therefore stigmatised); (3) mass produced culture that **exploits** ordinary consumers (a **Marxist** view and overlapping with **Consumer Culture**); (4) **authentic** culture created by ordinary people (also called **folk culture** and viewed as the opposite of Consumer Culture); (5) a negotiated culture that is imposed by the ruling classes but ordinary people are free to discard parts of it (an **Interactionist** view – see **Chapter 3**, p67); (6) a pick'n'mix collection of high and low cultural ideas that people can embrace or discard (a **Postmodernist** view you will learn more about later in the course). Storey's ideas show that Popular Culture is probably the hardest type to define: it means different things to different Perspectives.

TYPES OF CULTURE: CONSUMER CULTURE

Consumer culture includes cultural products that can be bought and are promoted through advertising. Consumer culture includes art like chart pop music, food like supermarket brands, clothing like fashion brands, sports accessed through subscriber-only channels and lifestyles involving shopping, surfing the Internet, visiting restaurants and hotels and wearing the latest fashions.

- Consumer culture can be expensive and this can make it **exclusive**; some consumer culture products are related to **High Culture**, such as designer jewellery, five star hotels, Michelin-starred restaurants that are beyond the budgets of ordinary people. However, often consumer culture is **inclusive** in that it is open to anyone who can pay.
- Expensive consumer culture is often **privileged**: it confers status on people who enjoy it or produce it. It marks you out as fashionable and elegant. Cheap consumer culture is **stigmatised** because it marks you out as lacking discernment: earing junk food, high street fashions, listening to radio-friendly pop music.

Some people reject consumer culture, preferring to buy products that are "authentic," "artisanal" or "hand-made" – often paying more for products that are unique rather than factory-made. Of course, these products are made by businesses and paid for with money, so they are still part of consumer culture, even though they appear not to be.

AO2 ILLUSTRATION: FAST FASHION

Fast fashion means clothing designs based on styles presented at Fashion Week runway shows or worn by celebrities that are put on sale immediately. Fast fashion allows mainstream consumers to purchase the hot new look or the next big thing at an affordable price.

Fast-fashion retailers might introduce new products several times in one week to stay on trend. *Zara* and *H&M* are two big sellers of fast fashion.

Fast fashion offers instant gratification for consumers. It lets ordinary people dress in fashions associated with **privilege**, but the low cost makes it **inclusive**. However, it has been criticised for contributing to pollution, waste and encouraging a "disposable" mentality where trendy clothes are bought and thrown away when the next trend comes along.

Research: Sweat Shops in Asia, pollution due to Fast Fashion, the link between fashion and eating disorders, plus sizes in fashion

RESEARCH PROFILE: BAUDRILLARD (1970)

Jean Baudrillard (1929-2007) is a thinker from the **Postmodernist** perspective you will learn about later in the course. Baudrillard thinks that we are living in a new phase of human society where 'you are what you buy' – you acquire your **Identity** (*c.f.* **Chapter 3**, p62) from the things you purchase, the fashions you wear, the celebrities you follow, the brands you support.

Baudrillard goes further, arguing that people nowadays respond to media images rather than to real things. He calls this sort of life lived through media images a '**Hyper Reality**.' He uses the word '**simulacra**' to describe media images that we find more satisfying than reality itself. An example might be the airbrushed and photoshopped models on magazine covers that we find more beautiful than *real* men and women.

Functionalists and **Marxists** join together in deploring the sort of society Baudrillard describes, which is inauthentic and unreal (so **Functionalists** hate it) and based on money and spending (so **Marxists** hate it – *c.f.* **Young**'s 'social bulimia' on p42*).* **Feminists** have mixed views. Hyper-reality might be a society where women are not judged by their gender; however, the sort of simulacra found in the media create unattainable body images that women (and increasingly men too) find impossible to live up to.

TYPES OF CULTURE: GLOBAL CULTURE

Global culture includes cultural products that are enjoyed all over the world. Global culture includes American pop music and Hollywood films, worldwide food like burgers and cola, global sports stars and celebrities and worldwide brands like Nike, Microsoft and Disney.

Global culture can be seen as a version of consumer culture that has taken over the whole world. However, some aspects of high culture have 'gone global' too, such as the lifestyles of the rich revolving around owning racehorses and yachts, enjoying European classical music and collecting fine art.

Global culture is often viewed as the successful exporting of American or European culture to less developed parts of the world. This is tied to **colonialism** – the way wealthy and developed nations rule and exploit less developed nations.

However, not all global culture is American/European in origin. Foods like noodles, curry and sushi have come out of Asia along with falafels from the Middle East and peri-peri sauce from Africa. Bollywood cinema has come out of India and K-Pop music out of South Korea. Global culture is a mix of influences.

Global culture produces different reactions. Some people embrace it as part of living in a more diverse and interconnected world. Other people worry that global culture is driving out local culture, producing a world that is **culturally homogenous**, with everyone living the same way and enjoying the same things with no variation. These people engage in **cultural defence**: they promote their own local culture, lifestyle and language and resist 'foreign' influences.

AO2 ILLUSTRATION: NETFLIX

Netflix was founded in 1997 as a DVD rental service but in 2010 it became an international service streaming movies and TV shows. Lots of popular 'box set' TV series and big budget movies are available for a monthly subscription: £6 for a basic package going up to £15 for high-definition quality on multiple screens. By 2021, Netflix acquired over 200 million subscribers worldwide and is watched in 20 different languages.

Netflix streams films that count as **High Culture** ('art house' movies, performances of ballet and opera) as well as **Popular Culture** (Hollywood blockbusters, the entire series of the hit sit-com *Friends*). The affordable subscription fee makes it part of **Consumer Culture**. Christophe Tardieu, the director of the French National Cinema Centre, described Netflix as *"the perfect representation of American cultural imperialism"* because it encourages everyone to watch or imitate the style of American shows, creating a worldwide media 'empire' based on American culture.

Research: the French film industry, Bollywood, Korean pop or drama, the impact of streaming services on film, the impact of Chinese audiences on Hollywood

RESEARCH PROFILE: GIDDENS (1999)

In his classic book **Runaway World**, **Anthony Giddens** discusses **de-traditionalisation** – where people question their traditional beliefs about religion, gender roles, etc. People often continue with traditional lifestyles, rather than actually changing them, but their cultures become unstable, because people are aware that there are alternative ways of living; they know that they can abandon their traditions if they want to whereas before Global Culture came along most people found abandoning traditions unthinkable.

When people **do** abandon their traditions, they develop a '**global outlook**' – for example, people in wealthy countries donate money to charities when the Media informs them about disasters happening on the other side of the world. Giddens calls this emerging global identity '**Cosmopolitanism**' (from the Greek *kosmos* meaning 'the world').

Some people react against Cosmopolitanism by going in the opposite direction, doubling down on their traditions and embracing religious fundamentalism or nationalism. Some people explain the election of Donald Trump as US President in 2016 or the UK voting for Brexit in the same year as examples of people rejecting a global outlook.

*Giddens' ideas will be looked at in more depth when you study Globalisation as part of **3A: Globalisation & the Digital Social World**.*

TYPES OF CULTURE: SUBCULTURES

Subcultures are groups who share the norms and values of mainstream (or dominant) culture, but who diverge from it in specific ways; they are a culture within a culture.

The most noticeable subcultures are youth subcultures, which are often based around music. Some subcultures have very striking fashions, such as Punks with aggressive appearances (spiked hair, piercing, torn clothing) or Goths with all-black clothing and makeup.

Other subcultures can be based around hobbies, like Geeks who enjoy comics, science fiction, fantasy and games. Other subcultures are based around politics, religion or moral concerns, such as Vegans. What makes them a subculture, rather than just a point of view, is that they adopt unusual lifestyles. For example, Vegans won't use any products acquired through animal suffering, such as woollen or leather clothing, as well as avoiding meat or dairy food.

Subcultures produce different reactions. Some people regard them as making society more diverse and multicultural. Other people worry that subcultures can isolate people – especially young people – from mainstream norms and values, possibly leading them into crime, drugs and mental health problems.

Research: a youth subculture (punks, goths, hippies, emos, chavs), an online subculture, veganism, gamers, deviant subcultures like Incel or QAnon

AO2 ILLUSTRATION: COSPLAY

The term 'Cosplay' was coined in 1984 and adapted from 'costume' and 'play.' It was used to describe fans arriving at science fiction, comics and movie conventions dressed as iconic characters from books and shows.

It became popular in Japan, based on characters from anime (Japanese animated films) and spread to America through hobby conventions for comics, cult TV and video games.

An important feature of Cosplay is that cosplayers create their own costumes, rather than hiring or buying pre-manufactured 'fancy dress' outfits.

Established cosplayers like **Jessica Nigri** earn money by appearing as characters from films and video games.

Cosplay is part of **Popular Culture** (since it's based around characters from comics, TV, films and video games). It has an odd relationship to **Consumer Culture** because cosplayers create their own costumes rather than buying them; however, it's strongly linked to the entertainment industry. Because it emerged from Japan and retains a strong link to Japanese anime, it could be seen as part of **Global Culture** too. When Western Cosplayers dress up as Japanese characters (or Japanese Cosplayers imitate Western characters like Disney princesses), that's an example of **Hybrid Culture**.

RESEARCH PROFILE: THORNTON (1995)

Another Sociology classic is *Club Cultures* by **Sarah Thornton**. Thornton takes **Bourdieu**'s idea of **cultural capital** (p19) and adds her own idea of **subcultural capital**. Having subcultural capital means being 'in the know' about the latest trends, products, artists or styles in your subculture.

Thornton looks at the '90s club scene where subcultural capital meant knowing where the hip DJs would be playing and the music that was authentic and original, as opposed to mainstream pop. Subcultural capital applies to other 'taste cultures' like fashion, gaming, art, film or celebrity gossip.

The arrival of social media has made Thornton's ideas even more relevant, as online creators with subcultural capital gain followers and become 'influencers.'

TYPES OF CULTURE: HYBRID CULTURE

Hybridity is an important idea that will be developed in **Chapter 3**. A hybrid is a mix or blend, so hybrid culture is a mixing of two cultures, like mixing yellow and blue to get green.

Hybrid cultures often emerge because of immigration. 2nd or 3rd generation immigrants (the children or grandchildren of people who move to a new country) grow up blending the culture of their family's background with the culture of the society around them.

Another type of hybrid culture happens when British people adopt the lifestyle, fashion or language of other cultures. **Antony Giddens (1999)** refers to this as **reverse colonisation,** which is when a powerful culture is changed by the cultures of the countries it once dominated. Examples would include the British passion for curries, Indian words entering the English language (like shampoo, bungalow or pyjamas).

Hybrid culture produces different reactions. Some people embrace it as part of living in a more diverse and interconnected world. Other people worry that hybrid culture is diluting the more authentic cultures it is blending together. These people engage in **cultural defence**: they promote their own local culture in (what they imagine to be) its 'pure' form and resist 'foreign' influences.

AO2 ILLUSTRATION: TIKKA MASALA

One in seven curries sold in the UK is a chicken tikka masala and in 2001 it was voted Britain's favourite dish, ahead of 'traditionally' British recipes.

However, the origins of tikka masala are unclear. Some say it came from the Punjab in India, other say it was invented in Glasgow in 1971.

It seems that Pakistani chefs came up with the dish to please British customers, so it's a case of British culture influencing Asian culture which then in turn influences British culture: a classic case of **global culture** at work.

Food Network UK (2011) surveyed 2000 British people and found that korma had knocked tikka masala off the top spot. Half of the respondents said that, having become accustomed to spicy food, they found traditional British dishes such as cottage pie, sausages and mash or fish and chips too dull.

RESEARCH PROFILE: BACK (1996), NAYAK (2003)

Les Back studied two London estates in the 1990s and found young people had developed a **Hybrid Culture**. It wasn't just the children of Caribbean immigrants who had mixed their islands' culture with the British culture; the White British youths had adopted Black fashion, language and style (such as a love of Hip-Hop music). Back calls this *"playing with different cultural masks."*

Anoop Nayak describes white youths adopting Black American hairstyles (dreadlocks), music (Rap) and language ("Yo"); he terms them **"White Wannabes"** (because they 'wannabe black').

In the early 2000s, the comedian **Sacha Baron-Cohen** created the character of **Ali G** to poke fun at this sort of Hybrid Culture; Ali G is a 'white wannabe' who speaks in a 'Jafakan' accent mixing British and Jamaican speech styles.

Baron-Cohen's comedy represents this sort of hybrid culture as inauthentic and silly: Ali G is very dim and his language and behaviour is a pose borrowed from celebrity rappers. Even the word 'Jafakan' suggests this sort of culture is 'fake.'

However, that's not the point that Les Back and Anoop Nayak are making. They claim that these Hybrid Cultures are completely authentic blends of White and Black culture..

AO2 ILLUSTRATION: MY CULTURE IS NOT YOUR PROM DRESS

My culture is NOT your goddamn prom dress.

In 2018 a Twitter storm erupted when Keziah, a 18-year-old American student posted photos of her prom, including herself wearing a Chinese style prom dress. Jeremy Lam, objected to these photos, tweeting: *"My culture is NOT your ... prom dress."*

The problem was that Keziah is not ethnically Chinese, so Mr Lam felt she had no right to wear these clothes. He accused her of **cultural appropriation** – effectively stealing from another culture in a disrespectful way.

When does **cultural hybridity** turn into **cultural appropriation**? One factor seems to be the relative privilege of the two cultures.

Poor white British youths can imitate Black British and American culture, but when the imitator is a privileged middle class White American, people feel uncomfortable with hybridity. These debates feature in **Chapter 3** when you will learn about **Intersectionality** (p63).

TYPES OF CULTURE: CULTURAL DIVERSITY

Cultural diversity is the characteristic of a society made up of a **plurality** of many cultures. The opposite would be a **monoculture**, where society only has a single culture.

There are probably no absolute monocultures, because there are always subcultures in a society, but some societies are more culturally diverse than others. **Chad** is an African country with 9 million inhabitants but made up of over 100 ethnic groups, each with their own language. It is the most culturally diverse country.

Multiculturalism (p17) is the policy of encouraging cultural diversity in a country. Supporters of multiculturalism claim that **cultural diversity** creates a richer and more sophisticated way of life, with a greater range of food, art, fashion and outlooks. Critics argue that multiculturalism creates division and competition between groups and can promote crime and violence as a result. They argue that **homogenous (monocultural)** societies are more successful.

Argentina is one of the most monocultural countries, with 97% of the population being White, Spanish-speaking and Roman Catholic.

Two approaches to multiculturalism are the **melting pot** and the **salad bowl** and *leitkultur* is an alternative (p17). Cultural diversity often leads to the emergence of **Hybrid Cultures**.

AO2 ILLUSTRATION: UYGHURS IN CHINA

The **Uyghur** (pronounced *wee-gur*) are an ethnic group of 12 million people living in western China, in the province of Xinjiang. The Uyghurs are culturally distinctive; in particular, they speak a language related to Turkish rather than Chinese and they are Muslims in a country that is officially Atheist but largely Buddhist or Confucian.

The Chinese government is accused of carrying out genocide against the Uyghurs. Genocide is defined by the United Nations as "intent to destroy, in whole or in part, a national, ethnical, racial or religious group." There are reports of Uyghurs being put into concentration camps, used as forced labour and sterilised to prevent Uyghur children being born. The camps are used to teach Uyghurs to abandon their own culture in favour of the dominant Chinese culture (called Han Chinese).

China admits that these re-education camps exist but denies genocide, claiming that the re-education camps are to combat terrorism. You must do your own research and decide if the treatment of the Uyghurs counts as genocide, but it *certainly* shows how opposed some states are to cultural diversity.

Research: the treatment of an ethnic minority (Uyghurs, Kurds in Turkey, Roma gypsies, Rohingya in SE Asia), the most culturally diverse countries (Papua New Guinea, Uganda) or cities (Toronto, Sao Paulo, Singapore).

EXAM PRACTICE: CULTURE

The OCR exam has three questions in **Paper 1 Section A**:

1. Explain, using examples, the concept of consumer culture. **[6 marks: 2 AO1 + 4 AO2]**

*This question asks you to give a definition then **two** developed examples. Developed examples will explain why they are examples of the thing you are defining, perhaps using sociological terminology. You should only spend 3 minutes on this question.*

2. Using sources A and B and your wider sociological knowledge, explain the concept of high culture. **[12 marks: 4 AO1 + 8 AO2]**

Source A	Source B
	Do you prefer listening to opera or rap? Do you like watching horse racing or wrestling? Do you read poetry or celebrity magazines? One type of entertainment is considered high and the other low. People often associate high culture with intellectualism, political power, and prestige. Some parents spend money to teach their children about high culture in order to give them advantages in life.

*Write **three** short paragraphs. The first explains the concept ('high culture' in this example). The second paragraph links it to Source A (list the things you see in the picture and explain how they link to the concept). The third paragraph links to Source B using quotes. You could add a fourth point, using an example from your wider knowledge rather than the Sources (e.g. high culture food) – but don't overthink this. You should spend 8-10 minutes on this question.*

3. Outline and briefly evaluate the view that global culture is becoming more influential in modern Britain. **[20 marks: 8 AO1 + 8 AO2 + 4 AO3]**

*Write **four** paragraphs. The first three paragraphs support the argument in the question (e.g. the global culture is growing in influence) and the fourth argues against it (getting the AO3 marks). For example, you could write about the **Functionalist** idea of global culture replacing national culture, then the **Marxist** idea of global Capitalism, then finish off with **Giddens' theory of cosmopolitanism** (p24) but then argue that the national culture is still influential (e.g. Brexit or Scottish Independence). Allow 20 minutes for this question.*

CHAPTER TWO – SOCIALISATION

Socialisation means the way a person is trained to take part in society. This includes literal training – like how to use a knife and fork or how to buy things in shops – but just as important is the mental training in society's beliefs. Socialisation is how we pick up **norms and values** (p16), which means it is how **culture** is passed on from one generation to the next.

Children who do not receive any socialisation are known as **feral children**. These may be children who were abandoned or neglected by their parents. Feral children do not learn how to understand language, walk upright, control their bowel movements or their emotions. In many ways, they live like wild animals. Training feral children into social behaviour is very difficult after childhood has passed, which shows how important childhood is for socialisation to take place.

Positive Views of Socialisation

Socialisation is viewed by some people in positive ways. It enables children to grow into adults who can fit into society. We learn all our social behaviour this way: language, manners, beliefs, morals and how we are supposed to behave in public. Without proper socialisation, we grow up confused, unhappy and unable to fit in. Poorly socialised children will struggle at school and are easy victims for those who want to exploit them: abusive relationships, gangs, drug-dealers.

This positive view of socialisation celebrates the people and organisations that carry out socialisation: mostly parents and teachers, but also the police, religious leaders and community groups (like the Scouts or local Youth Clubs). These groups are seen as doing something positive for society by 'raising young people right.'

This positive view is typical of **Functionalists**.

Negative Views of Socialisation

Socialisation isn't always positive. Being raised to fit in with society can also be brain-washing and indoctrination. If society has evil practices (like slavery, racist attitudes or warlike aggression) then socialising children means raising them to believe in slavery, hold racist views and be enthusiastic about war. Societies need to change, progress and evolve, but socialisation means that each generation is raised to be the same as the one that came before. Positive changes happen in society when socialisation *fails*.

This negative view of socialisation is suspicious of the influence of parents, teachers, religious and community leaders and the police. Instead, it might celebrate revolutionaries and rebels who fight against the system. It might see a positive side to criminals, gangs and social outcasts or misfits.

This negative view is typical of **Marxists** and **Feminists**.

The Nature-Nurture Debate

Nature is the idea that important human characteristics are innate – which means, we are born with them. People who support the Nature-view are **nativists**. Characteristics like eye colour and freckles are clearly innate and caused by genes, but what about social behaviour?

Nativists argue that biology is a big influence on intelligence, morals, gender roles and social attitudes. This means it is natural for men to be competitive and women to be compassionate. Not every man will be competitive and some women might be more competitive than some men, but in the population as a whole these characteristics will express themselves regardless of how we raise our children.

Nurture is the idea that important human characteristics are socially constructed – which means, we learn them from society. People who support the Nurture-view are **social constructivists**. They argue that biology only has a limited influence on intelligence, morals, gender roles and social attitudes. This means that the only reason men tend to be more competitive and women more compassionate is that society has encouraged them to behave this way. If society expected different things from people, they would learn to behave differently.

Research into other cultures (such as **Margaret Mead**, p9, p32) strengthens the nurture argument, because if sexual behaviour and gender roles were entirely based on biology they would be the same all over the world.

However, it's not a matter of *either* nurture is true *or* nature is true. Both have an influence. The question is, which has the stronger influence and provides the better explanation.

All sociologists are on the Nurture side of the Nature-Nurture debate, but some go further than others. **Functionalists** recognise that there are strong and unchangeable influences from biology that socialisation cannot make a big difference to. They accept that culture can make us 'go against' our biology, but they think that cultures that do this won't progress and are more likely to fall apart.

Marxists and **Feminists** have a much stronger social-constructivist view and see society as being responsible for our behaviour with much less influence from biology. They recognise that dire warnings about 'going against human nature' have always been trotted out whenever reformers want to change traditional way of doing things and they don't believe biology places any meaningful limit on the societies humans can construct.

> **Research:** the similarities between identical twins, cases of feral children, the impact of genes on social behaviour, cultures with unusual norms & values

RESEARCH PROFILE: MEAD (1935)

Margaret Mead 's research among the tribes of New Guinea (p9) shows the importance of socialisation. The reason the **Mundugumor** were so aggressive and the **Arapesh** so peaceful is because they socialised their children differently. The switched gender roles among the **Tchambuli** is evidence for the **social constructivist** viewpoint that our gender roles might be much more to do with socialisation and much less to do with biology than is commonly thought.

RESEARCH PROFILE: MONEY (1975), COLAPINTO (1998)

John Money (1921-2006) was a New Zealand psychologist who pioneered research into sex and gender. 'Sex' here means the biological characteristics present at birth but 'gender' refers to social categories of behaviour as masculine or feminine. Money reported on a patient he referred to as **John/Joan**: a biological boy whose penis was mutilated in a medical accident soon after birth and whose parents decided raised as a girl. Money advised the parents not to tell the child that she was originally born male. Money believed that gender was entirely socially constructed and reported that Joan had grown into a happy and well-adjusted girl.

However, in 1997 the true story came out. Journalist **John Colapinto** revealed that 'John/Joan' was really **David Reimer** who had grown up as **Brenda**, believing himself to be female. He was deeply unhappy as a girl, rejecting feminine dress and company and bullied by other girls at school for not fitting in. When he attempted suicide in his teens, his parents told him the truth and he immediately changed his name to David and rejected future drugs and surgery to enable him to live as a girl.

Sadly, David's mental health suffered and in 2004 he committed suicide.

There's a lot more to this story (including allegations that Dr Money abused Bruce as a child) but it serves as evidence for the **nativist viewpoint** that gender roles are innate and cannot be changed by socialisation.

You will notice that Mead offers evidence that socialisation can change gender roles but David Reimer's story serves as evidence that socialisation has limits and biology is more influential. The debate continues …

*Please be aware that this is NOT a study into trans identities. David Reimer experienced gender reassignment as a baby and this did not happen by his own choice. Trans women are born as biological males (or perhaps assigned male identity) but transition when they become aware that their gender identity does not match their assigned sex: this was **not** the case for David Reimer. Do not draw faulty conclusions about trans people from this case study.*

Research: watch *Dr Money & The Boy With No Penis* – terrible title but a very good 1-hour documentary from BBC2 *Horizon*, available online

PERSPECTIVES ON SOCIALISATION

Views on the importance and value of socialisation go to the heart of what makes the Perspectives different and a lot of this turns on the position sociologists take on the Nature-Nurture Debate.

CONSENSUS PERSPECTIVE: FUNCTIONALISM

Functionalism is the view that **society has developed to reflect human beings' biological needs**. A lot of training, education and preparation is need before a young human is able to make a valuable contribution to modern society or find a successful place in it.

This focus on our biological needs means Functionalists tend more towards the Nature end of the **Nature-Nurture Debate** (p31) than other sociologists. They still think Nurture is important – they think it's *very* important – but they recognise that there are characteristic we inherit biologically that Nurture cannot fully change and society cannot entirely ignore.

Functionalists value the institutions that pass on culture through **socialisation**: the family, education, religion and art. This can make functionalists seem very sentimental. However, they think society is all about fulfilling our biological needs, so they think socialisation needs to focus on preparing young people to become successful workers in the economy. Because the best institutions are the ones that fit in with biological needs, functionalists tend to think some types of family, education or religion are better than others. For example, they often praise the nuclear family (parents and their children, living independently of the wider family) and they believe in separate roles for men and women (based on the idea of innate biological differences).

Citizens have to be socialised into **universalistic values** that are shared throughout society, not just the local values of their family, neighbourhood or ethnic group. If this is successful, people can 'rise to the top' through talent and hard work – the ideal of a **Meritocracy** (p60).

If socialisation goes wrong, humans grow up unhappy and maladapted. They lack the skills to be successful and often fall into a **deviant subculture**, devoted to crime, drugs or some other unproductive lifestyle (like being a couch potato in front of the TV all day). Ultimately, poor socialisation results in a state of **anomie** and eventual suicide.

Despite this optimistic view about society, functionalists admit that institutions and behaviour can become **dysfunctional** when they go too far. Because we are biological creatures, aggression and greed will always be a part of human nature, no matter how we are raised and educated. Functionalists think society needs to protect itself, using agencies like the police. The police and courts are viewed as serving society and functionalists tend to downplay the suspicion that these institutions might be biased or corrupt or serve the interests of a minority instead of everyone.

CONFLICT PERSPECTIVE: MARXISM

Marxism is a Conflict Perspective which rejects the idea that society reflects human biological needs. Marxists believe that **society is shaped by conflict between groups with different economic interests**: a ruling class that holds the wealth and power in society and a working class that is much more numerous but poor and powerless.

This rejection of biological needs means Marxists tend more towards the Nurture end of the **Nature-Nurture Debate** (p31) than other sociologists. For Marxists, economic relationships (who has wealth and power and who doesn't) are much more important than biology. They are very sceptical about the idea that any human behaviour is 'natural' or 'unnatural' and claim that a lot of things that seem 'obvious' to people only seem that way because a powerful **ideology** has brainwashed them into thinking so.

Marxists are suspicious of the institutions that pass on culture through **socialisation**: the family, education, religion and art. This can make Marxists seem very cynical. However, they think that people will be freer and more fulfilled if they can escape from the influence of traditional institutions and the **ideologies** they pass on.

Marxists see racism as another side effect of Capitalist ideology. The police and courts are viewed as serving the interests of the ruling classes rather than protecting ordinary people; these institutions are seen as biased or corrupt.

CONFLICT PERSPECTIVE: FEMINISM

Feminists believe that **society is structured in favour of the interests of males**: women are subordinated to men and are threatened with physical or sexual violence as well as **patriarchal ideology** to keep them in line.

Many Feminists reject the idea that gender is based on biology. The idea that women are 'naturally' timid or caring is **socially constructed** and nothing to do with hormones or ovaries. These Feminists believe it is important to challenge these damaging stereotypes about women and the **nativist** viewpoint underlying them.

Other Feminists would go a bit further towards the Nature viewpoint (a bit like **Functionalists**). They might acknowledge that there *are* biological characteristics that distinguish women and perhaps qualities like sensitivity and peacefulness that go with these, but they think that patriarchal society dismisses and devalues these qualities in favour of more stereotypically masculine ones like aggression and competitiveness.

Feminists are suspicious of the institutions that pass on patriarchal ideology through **socialisation**: the family, education, religion and art. However, they think that people (both women *and* men) will be much freer and more fulfilled if they can escape from the influence of traditional gender roles. For example, they often criticise the nuclear family for trapping women in the roles of housewives and mothers and passing on restrictive gender roles to children.

SOCIALISATION: A TOOLKIT

Socialisation is a process of raising people to join society and share its norms and values.

- Some socialisation is **explicit**, which means the people involved are aware of what's going on (such as when a parent punishes a child to make sure it behaves in the future).

- Other socialisation is more **implicit**, which means people aren't consciously aware of what they're doing (such as when a mother takes her daughter shopping with her or a father invites his son to watch a football match with him).

- Eventually, we **internalise** the socialisation process, which means we absorb its lessons and make them part of our personality, so that we do what we've been socialised to do (like shopping or watching football) without remembering that we were ever taught to do it in the first place.

The people who socialise us are the **agencies of socialisation**. Some of these know what they are doing and view it as their job (for example, social workers) but others only socialise us accidentally, while they are aiming to do something else (such as our friendship group, who might snub us when we behave badly).

The final concept is **social control**, which is how society deals with us when socialisation fails and we act against its norms or break the law. There are **agencies of social control** that intervene to bring us back into line and, again, some of these do this as part of their job (like the police) but others do it in a more casual way (such as your family giving you a 'talking to').

TYPES OF SOCIALISATION: PRIMARY SOCIALISATION

Primary Socialisation is the influence of your parents. It includes learning to walk, talk, use the potty, eat food correctly, dress appropriately and restrain antisocial impulses. It might also include reading and writing and basic religious practices as well as loyalty to sports teams and other family traditions.

Functionalists view Primary Socialisation as particularly important. **Talcott Parsons (1959)** describes fathers as **instrumental role leaders** who discipline the children while women are **expressive role leaders** who are caring; boys grow up to imitate their fathers and girls their mothers. In the 1950s, these gender roles were not controversial but even in the 1950s, Parsons was only really describing the lifestyle of middle-class families.

Eli Zaretsky (1976) is a Marxist who agrees that the family socialises children but thinks it does so for the benefit of Capitalist employers rather than the children themselves. The family trains up a new generation of workers: the sons imitate their fathers' unquestioning obedience to the ruling class and the daughters imitate their mothers by devoting themselves to helping their husband be a good worker.

*This is a pretty good illustration of the difference between two Perspectives. Functionalists think it's in **our** benefit to be socialised and join the workforce, but Marxists think the Capitalist bosses are the ones who **really** benefit.*

AO2 ILLUSTRATION: GENIE

Genie Wiley was 13 when she was rescued from her abusive family by social workers in 1970. She looked 6. She had been strapped to a chair in an upstairs room by her father and left there since she was a toddler. If she made any noise she was beaten. Genie had never learned to speak, chew food, straighten her arms or legs or use the potty. She had never experienced human affection or any sort of intellectual stimulation in all that time.

Although cared for by social workers and studied by psychologists, Genie made only limited progress in learning to interact with people. After learning a few words, she was returned to her mother, then to foster homes, where she was abused again and stopped speaking altogether. Her true identity was kept secret to protect her.

Genie is a 'feral child' and strong evidence for the importance of primary socialisation during the 'critical period' of early childhood.

Although offered here as AO2 application of sociological concepts, the case of Genie could also be used as AO1 sociological knowledge and understanding. Searching the Internet will turn up many videos and websites about Genie and other feral children.

Research: evidence for a 'critical period' for socialisation in childhood, outcomes for other feral children (e.g. Oxana Malaya, Sujit Kumar, Andrei & Vanya the Czech twins, Isabel Quaresma)

TYPES OF SOCIALISATION: SECONDARY SOCIALISATION

Secondary Socialisation is the later influence of other people on your social experience. Children are influenced by their teachers, but also by youth leaders, religious leaders and later by employers. Peer groups (friends) and the media (TV, the Internet, pop music, video games) also affect our norms and values. The socialisation that continues into adulthood (for example, in the workplace) is sometimes termed **Tertiary Socialisation** (tertiary means "third").

Functionalists have the same positive view of Secondary Socialisation. **Talcott Parsons (1959)** argues that the family teaches children **particularistic values** but Secondary Socialisation teaches **universalistic values**. Particularistic values are the particular attitudes of your family – how things are done in your home. Universalistic values are broader values common in society. For example, your family might teach you to apologise to your sister after being mean to her but in society you are expected to apologise to total strangers if you accidentally bump into them. This is going from the particular (be nice to your sister) to the universal (be nice to people generally).

Marxist sociologist **Louis Althusser (1970**, p51**)** argues that the ruling class maintain power by using the **Ideological State Apparatus (ISA)**: institutions that spread ruling class ideology. Schools are part of the ISA: they prepare pupils to accept a life of exploitation under Capitalism.

*Another difference between two Perspectives. Functionalists think Secondary Socialisation is for **our** own good, but Marxists think it's really a type of brain-washing.*

AO2 ILLUSTRATION: BRITISH VALUES IN SCHOOLS

Since 2014, schools in the UK have a responsibility to teach British values as part of the curriculum (usually through PACE, PSE or Guidance but also through other subjects or Form Time). This includes teach students about democracy, tolerance, respect for other religions and freedom of speech. This is a good example of schools socialising children into **universalistic values** that they might not learn from their families.

Some critics complain that these universal values are in fact too **particularistic**: they are too limited and in a **Global Culture** we should be teaching global, rather than British, values, such as human rights and concern for the planet's environment. **Marxists** see the focus on Britishness as an example of the **ISA** in action: teaching the working classes in the UK to see themselves as different from the working classes in other countries.

Research: the *One Britain One Nation* song proposed for UK schoolchildren, what is taught as part of British values in schools, what other countries teach about their values in schools

AGENCIES OF SOCIALISATION

Agencies are groups of people or actual organisations that carry out socialisation. Sometimes socialisation is their explicit purpose (for example, teachers teaching British values, *above*) but other agencies do their job without realising it.

SOCIALISATION BY THE FAMILY

The family is the main agency of **Primary Socialisation**. For **Functionalists**, this is particularly important work. Case studies like **Genie** (p36) suggest that childhood is a critical period for receiving important socialisation. If the family does not do its job properly, poorly socialised children will become dysfunctional adults, leading to a lack of **social solidarity** and creating **anomie**. Functionalists often link crime, gang violence and drug abuse to poor Primary Socialisation.

Marxists and **Feminists** are more suspicious of the family and see it as an agency that passes on negative values, like respecting Capitalist bosses or expecting women to have a subordinate role.

AO2 ILLUSTRATION: KIBBUTZIM

A *kibbutz* is a type of commune found in Israel where adults live together, farming the land and sharing the work and the profits. Life in the kibbutz is very egalitarian, with males and females sharing the work.

Children in a kibbutz (the plural is *kibbutzim*) live together in a children's house. The adults take it in turns to care for them and the children might not have much contact with their biological parents; instead, the entire community is like a parent to them.

Kibbutz-children do not grow up damaged by this, which shows that **Primary Socialisation** does not have to be done by your literal parents, so long as it is consistent and caring.

Kibbutzim make the same sort of point as **Margaret Mead**'s research in Samoa and New Guinea in the 1920s (p9) – that family arrangements are **socially constructed** and one type of family isn't better or more natural than another.

Research: the experiences of children who grew up on a Kibbutz, the experiences of Romanian orphans in the 1990s, parents who raise their children to be 'gender-neutral'

RESEARCH PROFILE: OAKLEY (1974)

Ann Oakley is an important Feminist scholar and novelist who wrote two important books in 1974: *Housewife* and *The Sociology of Housework*. Oakley shows how the family socialises children into traditional gender roles. This is done through: (1) **manipulation** (parents encourage or discourage behaviour based on the child's gender); (2) **canalization** (directing children to show more interest in certain toys, e.g. dolls or cars); (3) **verbal appellations** (the language parents use, e.g. pretty girl vs tough boy); (4) **different activities** (encouraging girls to play indoors and help with chores vs boys outside).

Oakley's research is from the '70s but is it out-of-date? Many parents make a greater effort today to raise their children in a **gender-neutral** way but the toy industry is still very **gender-coded** (with pink packaging for girls and blue for boys).

This ironic picture shows the cover of a game from 1967. The artwork represents the sort of

gender roles **Talcott Parsons** would be proud of: father and son relaxing with a (militaristic) game while the daughter imitates her mother with the housework – and everyone looks delighted with this arrangement.

This is a good example of Oakley's point about **different activities** for girls and boys.

It also shows how **Consumer Culture** (p21) influences socialisation, because people assume that the images on commercial products represent the **norms** of how things are supposed to be.

SOCIALISATION BY PEER GROUPS

Friendship groups are an agency of **Secondary Socialisation** because they reward socially acceptable behaviour (with popularity) and punish deviant behaviour (by snubbing you). This carries on right through life.

Of course, some peer groups *encourage* deviant behaviour. Many children first smoke or shoplift or truant because of encouragement from their friends. This can be because the peer group is actually a deviant **Subculture** (p24). The **Functionalist** sociologist **Albert Cohen (1955)** argues that working class children are likely to form such a subculture because of **status frustration**: when they realise they cannot compete with privileged middle-class children for success in school, they form a subculture with **anti-school norms and values**, where it's 'cool' to fail tests, get punished by teachers and skip lessons.

*Does it strike you as odd that a Functionalist links deviance to being poor? It shouldn't. **Marxists** would attack Cohen for painting an unfair picture of working-class children, who try just as hard at school as middle-class children – and middle-class children also have deviant habits but are perhaps better at hiding them.*

AO2 ILLUSTRATION: EVERYONE'S INVITED WEBSITE

When London student **Soma Sara** shared her experiences of sexual harassment at school on Instagram, she received hundreds of messages from girls with similar experiences. In 2021 she set up the **Everyone's Invited** website (**everyonesinvited.uk**) and quickly received over 10,000 testimonies of sexual harassment and rape. Mostly the testimonies were from girls at some of the UK's top private schools and the perpetrators were boys from some of the most privileged families. However, more testimonies are appearing from girls at state schools too.

Screen capture of the Everyone's Invited welcome page on 8/7/21

This shows that peer groups can socialise children into very antisocial behaviour and that this is not limited to just working-class children who do badly at school.

RESEARCH PROFILE: WILLIS (1977)

Paul Willis published *Learning To Labour*, based on studying a group of 12 working class schoolboys. Willis spend 18 months observing and interviewing the boys (he terms them 'the Lads') and their teachers and another 6 months studying them at work after they left school. Willis reports that the Lads were uninterested in school, saw studying as *"cissy"* (effeminate), only valued *"having a laff!"* (meaning disrupting lessons and vandalism) and looked forward to working in a factory instead.

As a **Marxist**, Willis links this to **ruling class ideology**: these anti-school peer groups socialise working class children into the mentality needed for a life of dead-end jobs.

*Willis' study of the Lads is fascinating and used unusual methods to gather data. We shall look at it in more detail later in the course in **2A: Research Methods***

SOCIALISATION BY THE MEDIA

Children encounter the media through nursery rhymes and bedtime stories, then through children's TV shows and video games, later through pop music and celebrities. They are also exposed to advertising, branding and online 'influencers.' This socialisation continues right through life, as adults consume sports, soap operas, game shows, lifestyle magazines and the news.

Functionalist often point out the positive functions of the media – informing us about the world and sharing positive messages. For example, children's TV shows often end on a moral message about safety, fairness or honesty and soap operas often contain storylines highlighting social problems and encouraging tolerant attitudes. **Marxists** and **Feminists** are more likely to complain about the biased and distorted views in the media, particularly the positive view of Capitalism in advertising and the lack of positive representation of women, minorities and the poor. Sometimes **Functionalists** complain about the media too, especially the excessive portrayal of violence or sexual content presented to children.

AO2 ILLUSTRATION: DOCTOR WHO AND ANNE BOLEYN

In 2017, **Jodie Whittaker** took over the role of time-traveling hero Doctor Who in the long-running BBC TV drama. Previously, the character had always been male and acted by men. Whittaker announced "Doctor Who *represents everything that's exciting about change*" but a minority of fans were unhappy, complaining that making the character female was being done for the sake of 'political correctness' (i.e. to cash in on the popularity of Feminist ideas).

In 2021, **Jodie Turner-Smith** played the 16th century Tudor queen in Channel 5's TV drama *Anne Boleyn*. As a black actor, Turner-Smith was unexpected casting, because the historical Anne Boleyn was white at a time when very few people of colour were present in English politics.

Marxists and **Feminists** tend to welcome this, because it challenges our assumptions about ethnicity and gender. **Functionalists** are more critical, because they want the media to present the truth about the world (historically, Anne Boleyn **was** white) and support traditional ideas about gender in particular.

You can find other examples of "colour-blind" casting (such as the TV series Bridgerton*) and examples of swapping the gender of famous characters (such as the Marvel superhero* Thor*).*

RESEARCH PROFILE: YOUNG (2007)

Jock Young is a **Marxist** sociologist who writes about the link between crime and poverty. Young points out that the media constantly bombards people with glamorous products and lifestyles they cannot afford. Even if people make enough to live con, they *feel* poor compared to what they see on the media. Even if they acquire expensive phones, fashions, cars or holidays, in next-to-no time these things are out-of-date.

Young calls this **social bulimia** – a comparison to the eating disorder that makes people want to binge eat then throw up what they've eat; we want to buy goods then discard them and buy more. Young argues a Capitalist society is a **bulimic society**, creating despair, envy and anger which leads to crime.

*Young links his ideas to another sociological Perspective called **Postmodernism**, which I will explore in **2A: Options**. Postmodernism has a lot to say about the influence of the media in society.*

SOCIALISATION BY RELIGION

The UK is an increasingly secular culture (one where religion plays little part in social relationships) but religion continues to be an agency of socialisation: there are Church of England, Catholic, Jewish and Muslim schools and church groups run Sunday Schools that combine fun and games with religious education. Christmas Carol Concerts are still popular and 40-50,000 people get married in a Church of England church every year. Some ethnic groups (like Eastern European Catholics or British Asian Muslims) have much higher rates of religious observance.

Religion socialises children by offering simple moral rules (e.g. the Ten Commandments) and role models (from Bible stories or the lives of saints). Adults are socialised because religion offers **rites of passage** through life's difficult transitions: ceremonies for the birth of children, marriage and funerals (jokingly summed up as "*hatching, matching and dispatching*").

Functionalists tend to approve of religion (in moderation) because religion produces **social cohesion**. Notice that this isn't the same as believing religion to be *true*; you can think religion is good for society even if God doesn't actually exist. **Marxists** criticise religion for offering a 'pie-in-the-sky' solution to social inequality and encouraging people to be obedient to the ruling class; **Feminists** see religion as passing down traditional gender roles that oppress women.

Religious extremism is a different sort of socialisation that goes against society's values and leads to deviant behaviour. Functionalists tend to view extremism as a distortion of the true meaning of religion (which is, according to them, supporting society's values). **Marxists** sometimes see extremists as resisting Capitalism and **Feminists** sometimes see them as resisting Patriarchy; for example, **Leila Ahmed (2011)** is a Muslim Feminist who argues that the veil helps Muslim women resist Patriarchy because they are not judged by their bodies.

AO2 ILLUSTRATION: THE BURQA BAN

Few religious traditions are as controversial as the Islamic women's veil. Different groups of Muslims interpret the veil differently, from simple head scarves (*hijab*) to full face coverings (*burqa*). In 2011, France became the first European country to ban wearing full-face veils in public, on penalty of a fine. Previously, in 2004, France banned the wearing of Muslim headscarves (and other "conspicuous" religious dress) in schools.

France has the largest Muslim population in Europe but the majority agree with the government when it describes the face-covering veil as *"contrary to the values of the republic"* (a very **Functionalist** point of view).

Critics claim the ban goes against personal freedom and is motivated by racist Islamophobia.

The Burqa Ban is an example of the France government trying to limit (possibly extremist) religion as an agency of socialisation.

However, in the UK, the focus is on the positive messages religions teach, so (non-extremist) Muslim schools with Muslim dress codes are encouraged. In 2005, a British schoolgirl Shabina Begum won a court case to be allowed to wear Muslim dress to her non-Muslim state school, even though it went against the school's dress code. She said: *"Today's decision is a victory for all Muslims who wish to preserve their identity and values despite prejudice and bigotry. It's amazing that in this so-called free world, I have to fight to wear this attire"* (source: *The Guardian*).

RESEARCH PROFILE: MALINOWSKI (1954), PARSONS (1964)

Branislaw Malinowski (1884-1942) went to **New Guinea** (just like **Margaret Mead**, p9) and studied the **Trobriand Islanders** who he thought preserved a 'pure' form of religion. The Trobrianders had religious rituals from stressful life changes like birth, puberty, marriage, illness and death; they also used rituals before going on dangerous sea-fishing expeditions. He argued that religion brings people together in times of stress, creating social cohesion.

Talcott Parsons (1965) took Malinowski's ideas and showed how Christianity helps people in the USA integrate into society and make sense of a confusing and contradictory world (for example, when there is injustice and unfairness).

This is a classic Functionalist view that modern Christianity is really just the same sort of thing as tribal religion; what matters is not any particular beliefs about God or Jesus but the **function** *of these beliefs – how they help people live in society.*

Marxists don't agree that religion helps people make better sense of the world: they see it as **false consciousness**, a sort of hallucination that keeps people out of touch with reality.

SOCIALISATION BY EDUCATION

School is the main agency of **Secondary Socialisation**. Schools teach skills and knowledge that is too advanced for many parents to pass on (such as science or complex mathematics or foreign languages) as well as the **universalistic values** students need to live in society.

Functionalists believe education works as part of a **meritocracy** (p60) Schools hand out qualifications based on talent and hard work and society rewards people according to their qualifications, paying higher wages and giving more prestige. **Marxists** point out that people are encouraged to *think* that their low status in society is their own fault (because they did poorly at school because of stupidity) whereas it is *really* because of how unfair and unequal Capitalism is.

AO2 ILLUSTRATION: RAISING OF SCHOOL LEAVING AGE (ROSLA)

Attending school up until the age of 10 became compulsory in England & Wales in 1870 and the school leaving age was raised to 15 in 1944, then 16 in 1972 and then 18 in 2018. Keeping young people in school (or college or in an apprenticeship) until they are 18 hugely increases the power of educational institutions to socialise them.

Functionalists believe that, as society becomes more complex, young people will require longer and longer periods of socialisation to prepare them to take a valuable role in it. However, some object that people aged 16+ should have the freedom to choose what to do with their lives (after all, they can choose to have sex and start a family but not to leave education!). **Marxists** complain that the extended education often involves gaining worthless qualifications which do nothing to improve inequality and poverty in society.

RESEARCH PROFILE: BOWLES & GINTIS (1976)

Bowles & Gintis studied schooling in America from a **Marxist** perspective. They pointed out that, alongside the **formal curriculum** (Science, Maths, History, etc) schools taught a **hidden curriculum** of norms and values that would turn students into obedient workers in a Capitalist society. Unlike the formal curriculum, the hidden curriculum isn't written down in any school brochure and most of the time teachers aren't even aware that they are teaching it to students.

Bowles & Gintis argued for the **Correspondence Principle** that claims that everything learned in schools corresponds to experiences in work, such as: (1) **Accepting Hierarchy** (accepting the authority of teachers and head teachers leads to accepting the authority of bosses); (2) **External Rewards** (qualification in school, wages in work, rather than pleasure or personal interest); (3) **Fragmentation of Knowledge** (separate school subjects, work involving a tiny part of production rather than understanding the whole thing).

*This is a classic **Marxist** view of school as a sort of factory churning out brainwashed children. It works well alongside **Willis'** Learning To Labour study (p41), but does it describe education today, in a society where most school-leavers don't work in gigantic factories?*

Functionalists would *agree* that education corresponds to the workplace, but they would disagree that this is a bad thing. Functionalists think it's good that education prepares people for work, because they don't accept that Capitalist society is fundamentally wrong or harmful.

Research: the debate over Grammar Schools vs Comprehensives, setting or streaming in schools, Summerhill school where there are no compulsory lessons, de-colonising the curriculum in schools

SOCIALISATION IN THE WORKPLACE

The workplace is the main agency of **Secondary Socialisation** (or perhaps Tertiary Socialisation) for adults. In the workplace, you are expected to be punctual, follow rules, dress to a code, meet deadlines and respect superiors. If you don't follow the rules, you are disciplined, demoted or sacked.

Functionalists view the workplace as another type of **meritocracy**, with promotions and pay rises rewarding talent and hard work. They worry that long-term unemployment leads to socialisation 'wearing off' adults, creating social problems like crime and drug abuse.

Marxists see the workplace as a much more exploitative place that exists to create profits for the Capitalist ruling class; they have a more positive view of the unemployed who they see as casualties of Capitalism and not a danger to society.

Feminists similarly view the workplace as a place of sexism, harassment, and inequality, with a **'glass ceiling'** that prevents women getting to the top jobs.

AO2 ILLUSTRATION: WORKING FOR AMAZON

Amazon is a **Trans National Corporation** (**TNC**) that is a giant in online shopping. Its warehouses ("fulfilment centres") are each the size of a dozen football pitches where workers sort products as customers order them.

In a 2013 BBC *Panorama* documentary, Adam, an undercover reporter at *Amazon*'s Swansea warehouse, described working 10½ hour shifts, walking 11 miles in that time, picking up an order every 33 seconds.

His work was controlled by a scanner. It instructed Adam where to go in the warehouse and told him how long he had to get there.

Adam said: *"We are machines, we are robots …We don't think for ourselves, maybe they don't trust us to think for ourselves as human beings."*

Amazon however says its workers are not exploited and they're proud of their safe and positive workplace. *Amazon* employs 55,000 people across the UK and 1.3 million around the world.

It's common to criticise **Marxist** sociology from the '60s and '70s (e.g. **Bowles & Gintis**, *above*) for being out-of-date because most people no longer go to work in gigantic factories. The UK is now a 'service economy' where people are more likely to work in shops, food outlets or warehouses. But the *Amazon* workplace seems to have many of the oppressive and dehumanising features of the old factories.

RESEARCH PROFILE: MARX (1844)

Karl Marx (1818-1883) was one of the founders of Sociology. He argued that work is supposed to be fulfilling for people and *was* fulfilling when workers made things for themselves and their community – making a table their family would eat off. However, Capitalism makes work unfulfilling when workers make things for strangers to own – and often don't make an entire thing anyway, they just make a part and never get to see the finished product (like a worker who just makes table legs and never sees a completed table). This leads to deep frustration and powerlessness, which Marx calls **alienation**.

Workers are not just alienated from their products under Capitalism: they are **alienated from themselves**. They feel de-humanised, just cogs in a big machine with no individuality; they don't matter because they can be fired and replaced. **Functionalists** have a similar idea (**anomie**, p10) but they think family, religion, etc. can compensate for it.

SOCIAL CONTROL: FORMAL AGENCIES OF SOCIAL CONTROL

Social order is the smooth running of society, with people following the rules. It involves shared norms about how to behave and the punishment of deviants to make them conform. Agencies of social control make this happen. **Formal social control** is very explicit: the people exerting the control know what they are doing and the people being controlled recognise it too. Deviance is usually defined by rules or laws that are written down and the punishments are public too.

CONTROL BY THE POLICE

The police are the formal agency of social control that most people encounter directly. In fact, they are the **only** formal agency of social control that many people have direct dealings with. The police have discretion in how they deal with law-breakers, from unofficial warnings ("Move along!"), to official cautions and arrests. The police supervise gatherings and sometimes using a technique called 'kettling' to contain protestors or rioters in an area of town. In the UK, the police are unarmed but firearms officers can be sent to deal with serious incidents.

Functionalists view the police as acting on behalf of ordinary citizens, doing the job of keeping society safe that we would otherwise have to do ourselves. This is consensus **policing** and a good example is the unarmed status of British police and how police officers can be approached to ask for help or even directions.

Marxists perceive **conflict policing**, with the police serving the interests of the ruling classes and being more interested in protecting property and businesses than helping ordinary people. They point out that the police disproportionately use powers to stop, search, harass and arrest working class people, especially ethnic minorities.

Feminists argue that the police are largely indifferent to crimes against women, being reluctant to investigate or record cases of domestic violence. They complain that women who report sexual assaults might be met with *"a culture of disbelief"* from the police (*The Guardian*, **2014**).

AO2 ILLUSTRATION: DEFUND THE POLICE

In 2020 in the US city of Minneapolis, **George Floyd** was murdered by a police officer, sparking protests and riots over police violence against Black Americans. One of the demands of the **Black Lives Matter** movement was to 'Defund The Police.' This means cutting the budgets allocated to police departments and spending the money instead on public services like housing, health and education.

Robert Reich (2020) terms this a focus on **social investment** instead of **social control**. Reich points out that the USA now spends more money on prisons than it does on schools. The idea is that, if people had better housing, healthcare and education, they would be more happy and secure and would not turn to crime, so less policing would be needed.

Defunding the police has a lot of support from **Marxists** (who believe that policing is excessive and oppressive) and **Feminists** (who believe women suffer particularly from cuts to public services and aren't well-served by the police).

RESEARCH PROFILE: WILSON & KELLING (1982)

Wilson & Kelling describe an experiment carried out in 1969 (by psychologist Philip Zimbardo) where a car was abandoned in a poor, high-crime district of New York and a similar car left in wealthy Palo Alto, California. Within hours the New York car had been vandalised and stripped of valuables, but a week later the Palo Alto car was still untouched. Then the researcher smashed the bonnet of the Palo Alto car with a sledgehammer. Within hours, it too had been vandalised – and by very respectable-looking people. The experiment shows that people react to signs of neglect in their environment.

Wilson & Kelling developed the **'Broken Windows'** theory from this: people respond to signs of disorder (like vandalism, graffiti, public drunkenness, littering) by becoming more deviant and criminal themselves. Therefore instead of focusing on big crimes police should show 'zero tolerance' for petty crimes; they should 'clean up the streets' and be a visible presence. When **Zero Tolerance Policing** was put into practice in New York in the 1990s, it went from being one of the most violent cities to one of the safest.

'Broken Windows' is a **Functionalist** answer to 'Defund The Police': it shows that police *do* contribute to social order, but not in the way you think; people become more law-abiding when they feel their neighbourhood matters.

However, 'Broken Windows' is controversial, because focusing on minor crimes means more police harassment of ordinary people. Moreover, other US cities showed big drops in violent crime in the '90s even though they didn't put Zero Tolerance Policing into action.

CONTROL BY THE LAW/LEGAL SYSTEM/COURTS

In free societies, **'rule of law'** is very important: this means the law should work the same way for everyone, what's a crime for a poor person should also be a crime for a rich person and no one should be able to get out of legal trouble by paying bribes, calling in favours or threatening their accusers. Crucial to this system is the concept of **'presumed innocence'** – no one should be treated as guilty until evidence proves them guilty. It's also important for the courts (the judiciary) to be separate from the government, so that judges can make independent decisions.

In practice, it isn't that straightforward. The law is much more concerned with **protecting property** and wealth than with protecting the poor. People have **unequal access to the law**. Having money to hire a good lawyer makes the difference between being found guilty or not guilty, the length of your sentence and the type of prison you go to.

Marxists argue that the law gives harsher punishments to poor people and pays less attention to **'White Collar Crimes'** carried out by the rich (e.g. tax evasion, fraud, polluting the environment**). Frances Heidensohn (1985)** is a **Feminist** who argues that women are accused of **'double deviancy'** in court: they are punished for breaking the law but their punishment is often harsher because they have also gone against gender norms by being rebellious. However, Heidensohn's argument has been challenged: in the UK, women are more likely to be cautioned than arrested, less likely to receive a prison sentence and receive shorter sentences on average.

AO2 ILLUSTRATION: BERNIE MADOFF

In 2009. businessman **Bernie Madoff** was sentenced to the maximum 150 years in prison for a fraud that wrecked the lives of thousands of people. The American judge Denny Chin said the *"breach of trust was massive."* When the sentence was read out, there was applause from his victims, who had described him as a *"thief and a monster."* Nearly 9,000 victims filed claims for losses because of Madoff's cheating. Madoff promised to invest money for his customers but spent it instead, faking bank statements to look like he was managing $65bn (£38bn) of investors' money, but in reality there was just $1bn left.

Marxists claim there are a lot of **white-collar criminals** (p49) like Bernie Madoff out there, but it is unusual for them to be caught and punished. Marxists argue that the money stolen and the lives ruined by this sort of crime is enormous, but **Functionalists** argue that **'street crime'** like assault, mugging and theft accounts for more day-to-day misery for ordinary people.

RESEARCH PROFILE: SUTHERLAND (1949)

Edwin Sutherland coined the phrase 'white-collar crime' and defined it as *"crime committed by the more affluent in society, who abused their positions … for personal benefit.*

Sutherland argued crime was widespread throughout all sections of society: corruption in government and business, fiddling expenses, tax fraud and embezzlement. However, white collar crime gets little attention and most of the agencies of social control – particularly the law and the courts – focus on street crime and property crime.

Social control over white collar crime is weak because there is often no single identifiable victim; this removes the perception that offenders are doing anything harmful. White collar criminals normally have the resources to hide their crimes or escape punishment (they can afford good lawyers).

In a Capitalist society, **Secondary Socialisation** encourages aggressive and ruthless competition and this means the law does not punish white collar crime as much as working class crime.

Research: other famous financial scandals, Jeffrey Epstein or Harvey Weinstein, the debate over presuming the innocence of rape suspects and believing the victim, the George Floyd case, Hate Crime legislation

CONTROL BY THE GOVERNMENT & THE MILITARY

The government of a country is usually held responsible if social order breaks down due to crime, rioting or war. The military is a powerful agency of social control at the government's disposal. In a **liberal-democratic state**, the government is limited in the social control it can use, since the courts are independent, and the police must obey the law as well as enforce it (called **'rule of law'**). In a **totalitarian state**, the government controls the courts and the police as well as the military and anyone criticising the government risks arrest or even execution.

Marxists argue that even liberal-democratic governments use military force against their own citizens. For example, British soldiers patrolled the streets in Northern Ireland up until the 1990s. There are also **conspiracy theories** claiming that people who protest against or embarrass the British state risk being silenced by the Security Service (**MI5**) — students must work out for themselves if such conspiracy theories are likely to be true.

AO2 ILLUSTRATION: THE 77th BRIGADE

In 2015, the British Government formed the **77th Brigade** of the British Army to engage in **cyber-warfare**: a group of military hackers and social media activists who would work towards national security online. The Brigade uses *Twitter* and *Facebook* to influence people's views and behaviour. **David Miller (2019)** said that it is *"involved in manipulation of the media including using fake online profiles"* but the British Government argues that the Brigade is *"helping to quash rumours from misinformation, but also to counter disinformation."*

Is this sort of cyber-warfare necessary for national security because other countries are using bots and trolls to interfere with elections and spread scare stories? Or are **Marxists** right to fear that the government and military are using online Psy-Ops (psychological operations) against their own citizens?

RESEARCH PROFILE: ALTHUSSER (1970)

Louis Althusser (1918-90) is a French Marxist who studied the power of the Capitalist state. Althusser argued that the state enjoys 'hard power' based on the threat of violence: the police and the military together make up the **Repressive State Apparatus (RSA)**. However, Althusser believed no state could survive by controlling its population with force alone. There is also 'soft power' based on making people believe that the state cares about them and that they *ought* to obey it: this is the **Ideological State Apparatus (ISA)** that operates through religion, education and the media.

Althusser's ideas help explain what the government is doing with the **77th Brigade**; the military is part of the RSA but when it goes online to spread propaganda it is part of the ISA too. However, most **Functionalists** would not agree with Althusser's assessment that the government and the military are mainly about controlling their own citizens; they think that the military exists to defend citizens from external threats (but of course, Marxists point out this is *exactly* what the ISA *wants* you to believe).

SOCIAL CONTROL: INFORMAL AGENCIES OF SOCIAL CONTROL

Social order cannot work purely through **formal agencies of social control**: there just aren't enough police and soldiers to make us all obey all the time. Alongside these, there are **informal agencies of social control** which are less obvious: the people exerting the control don't realise what they are doing and the people being controlled don't notice it either. Deviance is usually defined by public opinion and the punishments are more subtle and hidden.

CONTROL BY THE FAMILY

Since they are the main **agency of Primary Socialisation**, your family have a big influence. Families reward children for being good and punish them for being naughty. Later in life, people are still nagged, manipulated and shamed by their families into behaving in socially-approved ways. People might be held back from getting into debt, quitting their jobs or ending their marriages out of concern for what their families would say.

The social control exerted by the family isn't always positive. Families also bully their members and control them through domestic violence. Some communities experience 'honour killings' when a young person brings shame on their family.

Feminists point out that women are more intensely controlled by their families than men and are much more likely to be the victims of domestic violence. The latest **UN figures (2017)** show that 137 women around the world are killed every day by a partner or member of their own family – a total of 50,000 women a year.

AO2 ILLUSTRATION: HERO MOM SLAPS RIOTING SON

During riots in the US city of Baltimore in 2017, a video of a mother slapping her rioting son went viral. On social media she was called *"mum of the year."* **Toya Graham** was videotaped pulling her son (Michael, 16) away from the crowd, smacking him in the head repeatedly, and screaming at him: *"take that ****ing mask off."* The police commissioner praised her saying: *"I wish I had more parents that took charge of their kids out there tonight."*

You can find videos of this on Youtube if you search mum+slaps+riot+son

RESEARCH PROFILE: PARSONS (1959)

Talcott Parsons is a **Functionalist** thinker you have already studied for his views on **Primary Socialisation**. Parsons thinks the family contributes to social control by **stabilisation of adult personalities**. Families provide emotional support for adults, enabling them to cope with the pressures of living in society. For example, by playing with children, adults get to act out the childish side of their own personalities in a harmless way. For men in particular, the family acts as a **'warm bath'** enabling them to de-stress before returning to the competitive world of work. The family is a safe haven.

Feminists criticise this view, because it explains what men get out of the family, but not how it benefits women to be offering emotional support for their husbands with no one to support them. Increasingly, women work a **'double shift'** (**Duncombe and Marsden, 1995**) by doing a paid job outside the home then having the main responsibility for housework and childcare in the home. If the women have to support the man emotionally as well, then that is a **triple shift**.

CONTROL THROUGH PEER GROUPS/SUBCULTURES

Peer groups control us in a similar way to the family, putting pressure on us to be socially conforming and excluding us if we misbehave. Even **subcultures** (p24) that seem quite antisocial (such as 'the Lads' studied by **Paul Willis**, p41) might actually be preparing young people to take their place in the Capitalist economy (Willis claims the Lads' anti-school behaviour was preparing them for boring factory work).

AO2 ILLUSTRATION: PUNKS

Punk was a music and youth fashion trend that appeared in the late 1970s. Punks adopted a shocking look, with hair shaved or shaped into spikes or fins; makeup was aggressive, often with facial piercings; clothing was torn leather, denim and plastic, often recycled from second-hand items.

Punk music (typified by **The Sex Pistols**) celebrated anarchy, offence and anger. During the Queen's Silver Jubilee in 1977, the Six Pistols had a Number 1 hit with their mocking version of *God Save The Queen*, which was banned by the BBC for comparing the royal family to "*a fascist regime.*"

Punks in Trafalgar Square, London, England 1989 (photo by spratmackrel)

The Punk Subculture seemed to be about anarchy, which is the opposite of social control. Some former-Punks remained involved in radical politics after Punk fashions ended, but many settled down to conventional lives; for them, Punk had been a youthful phase.

RESEARCH PROFILE: HEBDIGE (1979)

Punks were one of several **Spectacular Youth Subcultures** of the 1950s-1980s. These subcultures were studied by the **Marxism**-inspired **Centre for Contemporary Cultural Studies (CCCS)** in Birmingham. The CCCS was particularly interested in punks, whose fashion showed a DIY sensibility that was the opposite of buying fashion from shops. **Dick Hebdige** used the term **'bricolage'** to describe Punk culture, referring to the way it found new uses for old objects, such as dresses made from bin liners and piercings from safety pins. Punk music also celebrated rebellion and a rejection of mainstream values. The CCCS concluded Punk was a form of **resistance to Capitalism** by working class youths.

This argument ignores the fact that many punks were from middle-class backgrounds who weren't particularly deprived. Punk was promoted by fashion designers like **Vivienne Westwood** and music producers like **Malcolm McLaren**, so it might really have been a product of Capitalism rather than resistance against Capitalism.

*Hebdige's ideas are explored in more detail in **Section B (Youth Subcultures)** on p140.*

CONTROL THROUGH THE MEDIA

The Media means everything that communicates information but it's usually short hand for **'the Mass Media'** which means everything that is recorded or published: TV, film, radio, newspapers and magazines, books, billboards and of course the Internet.

The Media provides role models that influence behaviour, in terms of what they buy, how they look and what their aspirations are. For example, celebrities like Kim Kardashian inspire fashion and a (probably unrealistic) ideal body image.

The Media shapes society's norms. It's common for the news, soap operas and online chat to reinforce norms about honesty, hard work and obeying the law. However, the Media can also reinforce deviant behaviour, such as video games glamorising violence or pornography making violence against women seem normal.

AO2 ILLUSTRATION: RUPERT MURDOCH'S NEWS CORPORATION

Australian businessman **Rupert Murdoch** runs a **Trans National Corporation (TNC)** that controls news and entertainment media in many countries. News Corp publishes three British newspapers: the *Times*, the *Sunday Times* and the *Sun*. It owns the movie studio *20th Century Fox*, American *Fox TV* and the Asian *Star* channels, the *Wall Street Journal*, the *New York Post* and 146 newspapers in Australia and *HarperCollins* book publishers.

Many people are concerned about the influence of Murdoch's media empire, particularly because he uses it to support his (right wing) views. For example, *Fox TV* supported Donal Trump as US President and *The Sun* supports the UK Conservative Party. News Corp is accused of influencing election results and referendums (such as the **2016 Brexit Referendum**). **Andrew Neil**, who edited *The Sunday Times* for Murdoch, claimed that Murdoch effectively the *"editor in chief"* of *The Sun* and intervened in how *The Times* and *The Sunday Times* reported some stories.

The 1992 headline where The Sun took credit for the UK General Election victory by the Conservatives.

RESEARCH PROFILE: MILIBAND (1973)

Marxists claim that the owners of Media corporations order journalists to put across particular messages which spread ruling class ideology: values that justify the privileges of the elite. This is what **Althusser (1970)** called the **Ideological State Apparatus (ISA)**.

Ralph Miliband agrees that the media shapes how we think about the world and that audiences are rarely informed about important issues, such as poverty and inequality. The Capitalist system is rarely challenged, and only pro-Capitalist views are presented. Journalists depend on the owners for their jobs so, even if there seems to be **freedom of speech**, they end up helping to spread **ruling class ideology**.

Functionalists take a **pluralist** view that there are lots of different viewpoints in the Media. Media-owners cannot influence *every* story published and are more interested in making money than getting their own political views across. They also think that **Journalistic Ethics** means that editors and journalists will resist attempts by the owners to bully them into conforming. Functionalists think the news media can be trusted to give us a balanced view of society – for example, *The Guardian* is a UK newspaper that challenges Capitalism, draws attention to inequality and opposes the views found in *The Sun*.

CONTROL THROUGH THE WORKPLACE

Paid employment plays a major role in most people's lives. A new worker must learn to conform to the norms of the workplace and usually internalises its values too. Those who do not fit in face **sanctions** which can be **informal** (being snubbed by your colleagues) or **formal** (demotion, possibly being sacked). This process of learning new norms and values in a new setting is called **re-socialisation**.

Res-socialisation isn't always a good thing. Some workplaces have toxic values. **Young (2007)** discusses **'social bulimia'** brought on by a culture that is obsessed with money and material possessions; **Sutherland (*White Collar Criminology*, 1949)** identifies **white-collar crime** that can be normal in some workplaces and **Althusser (1970)** identifies the workplace as part of the **Ideological State Apparatus (ISA)** that supports Capitalism.

The workplace is largely an **informal agency of social control** through peer pressure from workmates and bosses. For example, bosses sometimes study their employees' social media accounts so there can be consequences at work for deviant behaviour out-of-work. However, rules about things like bullying, sexual harassment, discrimination and Health & Safety amount to **formal social control** too.

Research: online campaigns to cause people to lose their jobs for Hate (or the 2020 invasion of the US Capitol building), Google sacking James Damore in 2017, failure of social control at work (eg. 2021 murder of Sarah Everard by a police officer)

AO2 ILLUSTRATION: LONG TERM UNEMPLOYMENT

Unemployment (which doesn't include people who are sick or in education/training) has risen and fallen over the years. The graph below shows how the late-1970s and early-'80s was a time of worsening unemployment (*cf*. **Punks** on p53), with similar periods of job losses in the mid-'90s and after **the Global Financial Crisis** of 2008.

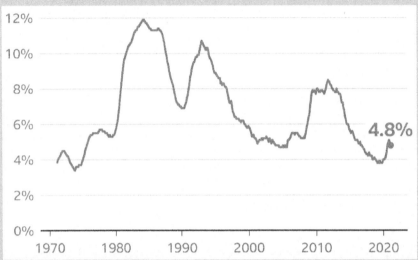

UK unemployment rate, showing percentage of people aged 16+ who count as unemployed up to March 2021 (source: ONS & BBC)

During this time, the UK has changed from an industrial economy (with many people losing their jobs working in factories) to a service economy (with many people now working in leisure, shopping and tourism). The changeover brought with it periods of high unemployment.

For a lot of people, unemployment is temporary. Official statistics suggest that there are only 2% of households where no adult has ever worked. The **Labour Force Survey (LFS)** was used by **Lindsey Macmillan (2011)** to examine two generations of worklessness: she estimated there were 15,300 'never worked' households in the UK. These tend to be homes where young people have only recently left education or where there is lone parenting, caring and illness.

Sociologists disagree on the impact of unemployment on social order. **Functionalists** argue that unemployment weakens socialisation and promotes anomie, leading to substance abuse and suicide. Some sociologists go much further than this, arguing that worklessness creates a subculture of deviance: sexual promiscuity, fatherless children, petty crime and fecklessness (dangerous irresponsibility).

Marxists argue these negative stereotypes are just **ruling class ideology** making the poorest people look like menaces when in fact they are the victims of Capitalism.

RESEARCH PROFILE: MURRAY (1984)

American scholar **Charles Murray** visited the UK during a period of peak unemployment in the 1980s and warned about the emergence of a new **'underclass'** of people who **never** worked came from families of **generational unemployment** (where the parents and the grandparents had never worked). These people lived entirely on benefits and Murray warned that they experienced broken homes, with boys joining gangs and girls becoming pregnant without long-term partners.

Murray claimed: *"Boys without fathers tend to grow up unsocialised. They tend to have poor impulse control, to be sexual predators, to be unable to get up at the same time every morning and go to a job."*

Murray recommended taking away benefits, forcing the underclass to return to the workplace where they would be **re-socialised**.

*Murray's views are hard-core even for **Functionalism**. He represents the ideas of the **New Right**, a Perspective you will study in **Section B (Youth Subcultures)** on p129..*

Murray's ideas are attacked for lacking evidence. The **Joseph Rowntree Foundation (2012)** studied deprived neighbourhoods in Glasgow and Middlesbrough and found that families where parents and their children had never worked were very rare, there was no evidence of **'a culture of worklessness'** and children were keen to find work even if their parents were unemployed.

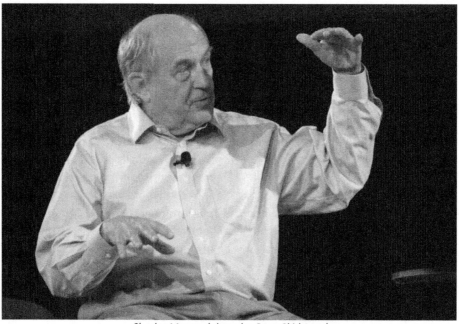

Charles Murray (photo by Gage Skidmore)

CONTROL THROUGH RELIGION

Religion used to hold a lot of influence over the norms of British society but secularisation is a process where religious institutions lose social significance; in 2019 church attendance was 854,000 each week, a fall of 300,000 from 2009. Nonetheless, there are still religious schools and religious attendance is higher for some religions and festivals (e.g. carol services at Christmas).

Religion is a key part of **Althusser**'s **Ideological State Apparatus (ISA, p51)**. Althusser argues that religion has been replaced by education (*below*) as the main ISA in society today. Religion's **formal social control** has declined since the 16th century, when you could be fined for not attending church on Sunday. UK Blasphemy Laws were abolished in 2008 (2021 in Scotland). However, religion continues to be an **informal agency of social control**, through sermons and community pressure to conform.

AO2 ILLUSTRATION: FAITH SCHOOLS

The first schools in the UK were part of the cathedrals and monasteries of the Roman Catholic Church in the Middle Ages. Later, the Church of England set up its own network of schools. Today, most church schools are 'voluntary aided' which means they are state schools with a distinctive **Church of England** or **Catholic** ethos (e.g. worship in Assembly, Bible study). The first UK **Muslim** school was founded in 1998, the first **Sikh** school in 1999 and the first **Hindu** school in 2008. In the UK in 2014, over a quarter of all primary-school pupils were educated in a faith school.

'**Faith school**' can cover a Church of England primary school with an ethnically mixed intake to a single-sex Muslim academy where pupils wear a hijab or a Catholic private school that non-Catholics want to get their children into because of its exam results.

RESEARCH PROFILE: DURKHEIM (1912)

One of the founders of Sociology is **Émile Durkheim** whose *Elementary Forms of Religious Life* explores the positive functions that religion has for society (regardless of specific religious beliefs). (1) gives **meaning and purpose** to life; (2) strengthens **social solidarity** by giving people a common set of beliefs and bringing people together physically for ceremonies; (3) strengthens **social order** by teaching moral behaviour (e.g. the Ten Commandments); (4) offering **comfort** to people in times of distress and promoting **physical health** (e.g. by discouraging drugs and casual sex); (5) motivating people to work for **positive social change** (such as peace campaigns, charity work, civil rights, etc.).

Durkheim is criticised for taking too optimistic a view about religion, which also fosters conflict and intolerance in society (e.g. **sectarianism** which is discrimination against one religion by another religion).

Marxists accuse religion of supporting the Capitalist *status quo* in society. In fact, Marx famously described religion as *"the opium of the people"* (1843) because, like opium (a powerful pain-killing drug) it brings them illusory happiness by preventing them from understanding what's really going on in society.

Feminists accuse traditional religion of spreading a negative view of women and restricting their freedoms; for example, many religions teach that women are more prone to temptation (justifying giving them fewer freedoms to work and study) or else women act as a temptation to men (justifying male abuse of women unless they act and dress very modestly).

CONTROL THROUGH EDUCATION

In school, students are sanctioned by **formal** and **informal social control**. Formal social control is through **school rules**: when they are broken, official sanctions are applied (detention, expulsion). Informal social control is sanctioning through a verbal warning by a teacher, with good behaviour is encouraged by praise from a teacher. This informal social control influences the pupil into a particular lifestyle and culture.

Bowles & Gintis (*Schooling in Capitalist America*, 1976) argue that the informal **'hidden curriculum'** (p45) influences students to accept Capitalism. Education is a key part of **Althusser**'s **Ideological State Apparatus (ISA, p51)** and **Pierre Bourdieu** (p19) argues that education leads to social reproduction, making sure each new generation stays in the same position as its parents, which is the *opposite* of **Meritocracy** (p60).

Back to school (photo: Phil Roeder)

AO2 ILLUSTRATION: MERITOCRACY

Meritocracy describes the process where jobs and pay are based on talent and achievements. The alternative to meritocracy is to reward everyone equally regardless of talent and ability (an idea pioneered by **Communism**) or to reward people based on social status (with wealth and privilege going to royal families and their favourites, which is an **aristocracy**).

Education is an important part of Meritocracy, because the qualifications you get at school, university or through training dictate the jobs you can do and the pay you deserve. The idea is that the most intelligent and hard-working students get the best qualifications and therefore the best jobs. This helps explain why a Capitalist society with very unequal wealth might still be just and fair.

This view is complicated by private schools (or 'public schools' as they are termed in the UK, rather confusingly). **Elitist Britain (2019)**, a study by the **Sutton Trust**, found that privately educated people dominate elite jobs in business, the arts, sport and politics, where 39% had a private education, compared with 7% of the general population. Football was the only major sport where the privately educated were underrepresented (5%).

RESEARCH PROFILE: DAVIS & MOORE (1945)

The Functionalist case for Meritocracy is explained in **Davis & Moore**'s *Some Principles of Stratification*. Stratification means the 'sifting & sorting' that places people in different jobs and in different income brackets.

For society to function well, jobs need to be done by the people most capable of doing them, who have been through the necessary training, who take the job seriously and do it properly. Society pays more for **functionally important jobs** that require more training or effort. This is why there are unequal rewards, so that ambitious individuals will compete with each other to get those rewards.

Critics argue that the most functionally important jobs don't actually get the highest pay. Why are bankers paid more than nurses? While it's obvious that some people are really good at (say) football, it's not so obvious that people who are CEOs of big companies have a talent for anything in particular.

Feminists point out that there is a **gender pay-gap** between males and females, even though women are just as capable of doing those jobs. The gender pay-gap in the UK in 2020 was on average 15.5%, although it has been falling since 2016 (source: **ONS, 2020**).

Research: social mobility in the UK, students from private schools in top jobs, unemployment among graduates, the gender pay-gap, the earnings of CEOs

EXAM PRACTICE: SOCIALISATION

1. Explain, using examples, the concept of primary socialisation. **[6 marks: 2 AO1 + 4 AO2]**

*This question asks you to give a definition then **two** developed examples. Developed examples will explain why they are examples of the thing you are defining, perhaps using sociological terminology. You should only spend 3 minutes on this question.*

2. Using sources A and B and your wider sociological knowledge, explain the concept of the nature-nurture debate. **[12 marks: 4 AO1 + 8 AO2]**

Source A

Source B

Parenting is the most important and challenging job any of us can have; yet, it receives little support in our society. There is very little formal training for this task and parents are often isolated and without adequate support networks. People often wonder why parents attend parenting education classes. Isn't good parenting innate? Studies have shown that in fact most parents can benefit from some guidance in order to do the best job they can in raising their children.

*Write **three** short paragraphs. The first explains the concept ('the nature-nurture debate' in this example). The second paragraph links it to Source A (list the things you see in the picture and explain how they link to the concept). The third paragraph links to Source B using quotes. You could add a fourth point, using an example from your wider knowledge rather than the Sources (e.g. feral children) – but don't overthink this. You should spend 8-10 minutes on this question.*

3. Outline and briefly evaluate the view that the police are an effective agency of social control. **[20 marks: 8 AO1 + 8 AO2 + 4 AO3]**

*Write **four** paragraphs. The first three paragraphs support the argument in the question (e.g. the police are effective at socialising us) and the fourth argues against it (getting the AO3 marks). For example, you could write about the **Functionalist** idea of the police enforcing society's shared values, then the **Marxist** idea that the police oppress the working classes, then finish off with **Wilson & Kelling's 'Broken Windows' theory** (p48), but then argue that scandals like the Stephen Lawrence murder and police racism have undermined their effectiveness. Allow 20 minutes for this question.*

CHAPTER THREE – IDENTITY

Identity means your self-concept or self-image: it's who you consider yourself to be. There are various **sources of identity** in society, such as gender, age, ethnicity and social class. These are **cultural characteristics**.

Identity at its simplest level involves **Self-Concept**. Each person has their own unique Self and the beliefs you have about yourself. Your Self-Concept is expressed in two ways:

- **Personal Identity:** the characteristics you ascribe to yourself – are you clever, funny, pretty, an introvert, good at sport, spiritual, kind to animals?

- **Social Identity:** the social groups you belong to (or people treat you as part of, whether you want them to or not) – are you White, middle class, heterosexual, male, disabled, teen-aged?

*In general, **Personal Identity** is studied by psychologists and **Social Identity** is more of interest to sociologists.*

Identity can be related to biology (and the **Nature** side of the **Nature-Nurture Debate**, p31). For example, ethnicity may be linked in some way to race and gender to your birth sex. But these links aren't completely fixed, because identity is also developed by **socialisation**: you learn what's expected of your ethnicity or gender and **agencies of socialisation** will reward you for conforming to these roles and stigmatise you for deviating.

For example, a girl who is a 'Tomboy' (aggressive, competitive, into masculine pastimes) deviates from social expectations of femininity. She might receive criticism from parents and teachers and be snubbed by peers. If she starts conforming by wearing dresses and showing an interest in stereotypically feminine pursuits, she might be praised and accepted by her peers. She might start to look back on her Tomboy experiences as "just a phase" and see herself as a conventionally feminine woman.

Identity could be viewed as what happens when the socialisation process is internalised and becomes part of your view of yourself.

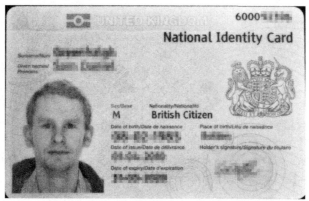

UK National Identity Card (photo: ZapTheDingbat)

Positive Views of Identity

These days, **Identity** is viewed as a very important characteristic. Indeed, some Identities are 'protected characteristics' and insulting or threatening people with those identities is a Hate Crime.

When footballer **Marcus Rashford** received racist abuse after a missed penalty in England's Euro 2020 Final, he defended himself by saying:

"my penalty was not good enough, it should have gone in, but I will never apologise for who I am and where I came from."

Rashford defends his **identity** as a Black British person whose family come from St Kitts in the Caribbean.

Other aspects of Identity that used to be considered unimportant or even stigmatised have become much more significant in the 21st century, such as being gay or trans or disabled or non-binary. There is a pressure for questionnaires and official statistics to represent these Identities and for language to change to present them in a positive light – such as encouraging people to indicate the pronouns they would like to be addressed with (he/his or she/hers or they/their).

Negative Views of Identity

Up to a point, all sociologists are interested in Identity and regard it as a positive thing. Rather like the **Nature-Nurture Debate** (p31), it's a matter of degree. The older sociological Perspectives are particularly interested in key Identities, but rather dismissive of others. For **Marxists**, your **Class Identity** is vitally important and paying too much attention to things like ethnicity and sexuality is a distraction from the all-important class struggle. **Feminists** view **Gender Identity** as central and are less interested (say) disability or nationality. Functionalists tend to attach a lot of importance to National Identity, since they view the nation state as the best political arrangement for creating social order and liberal democracy. In the past, Functionalists viewed some Identities (like homosexuality) as deviant and a threat to **social solidarity**, perhaps caused by **poor socialisation**.

Intersectionality

Intersection is the idea that you have more than one Identity; for example, footballer **Marcus Rashford** identifies as Black, British and working class. His Ethnic, National and Class Identities all *intersect*.

This is similar to the idea of **Cultural Hybridity** (p26) but intersection is different because cultural hybridity can be a blending where everything merges together whereas Intersection is about belonging to different social groups that remain distinct.

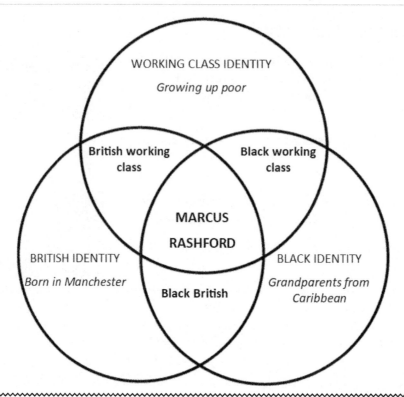

You have things in common with other people who share your intersecting Identities. New groups of **Neo-Marxists** ('neo' means new) and **Intersectional Feminists** are particularly interested in how some Identities are **privileged** and others are **oppressed**.

People who have intersecting privileged Identities (White, male, straight, cis-sexual, middle class) experience society very differently from those who have intersecting oppressed Identities (non-White, female, gay, trans, working class).

For these new Perspectives, privileged Identities replace the **Ruling Class**/the **Patriarchy** as the explanation for the inequality in society. Neo-Marxists now view **anti-racism** as just as much as part of opposing Capitalism as the class struggle; Intersectional Feminists see the struggle for women's rights as part of the struggle for the rights of non-White races and LGBT minorities.

Functionalists tend to be suspicious of this Intersectional view of society, because it suggests there is no **value consensus** for people with these oppressed Identities. Functionalists argue instead that people need to come together around values that are shared by *everybody* and they often propose National Identity as something that can do this. They oppose the tendency for people to 'splinter' into separate Identities.

RESEARCH PROFILE: CRENSHAW (1991)

Kimberley Crenshaw is an American lawyer and sociologist who introduced the concept of **Intersectionality** to **Feminism** (and then to other Conflict Theories like **Marxism**) in her article *Mapping The Margins*.

Crenshaw uses the example of a court case where a group of Black American women sued their employer, the manufacturer **General Motors** (GM), for discrimination, because promotions in the secretarial pool only went to White women. The court studied the issues of race and gender separately and rejected the claim; they pointed out that GM was not racist because it employed Black men in the factory and not sexist because it gave promotions to White women. Crenshaw points out how viewing Race and Gender separately misses the point that the women suffered from **'compound discrimination'** for their race *and* their gender. In effect, Black Women are doubly discriminated against, for being Black and for being women.

Crenshaw's ideas have been hugely influential as a way of analysing and opposing racism and sexism and has been extended to other oppressed identities too.

However, Crenshaw's ideas have been attacked for promoting a sense of victimhood rather than empowerment, by inviting all women and all Black people to consider themselves oppressed. Problems arise when different oppressed Identities come into conflict – for example, are lesbian women more discriminated against than Black women? **Kathy Davis (2008)** argues that intersectionality is ambiguous because of its "*lack of clear-cut definition*" but this very open-endedness is what makes it so successful and "*a good feminist theory.*"

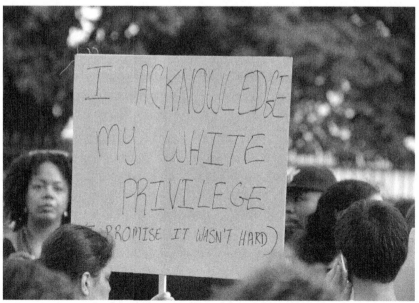

I acknowledge my white privilege (photo: afagen)

PERSPECTIVES ON IDENTITY

Perspectives are broad viewpoints but when it comes to Identity they fall into definite sub-groups, with traditional **Marxists** and **Feminists** resisting some of the implications of Identity and **neo-Marxists** and **Intersectional Feminists** embracing them.

CONSENSUS PERSPECTIVE: FUNCTIONALISM

Functionalists tend to trace part of Identity back to human biology. They also tend to think that it's healthy to conform to your biological identity. This means they tend to view **Gender Identity** as based on biological sex. They also regard **National Identity** as particularly important for integrating people around shared values. Because they believe in **Meritocracy** (p60), Functionalists do not accept that there are privileged and oppressed Identities: they think everyone gets a fair chance in society and inequality results from people having different talents and abilities, not privilege or discrimination.

Of course, Functionalists aren't idiots. They recognise that there **is** *discrimination in society. They just don't accept that it's widespread or that it explains every inequality that exists.*

CONFLICT PERSPECTIVE: MARXISM

Traditional Marxists don't agree with Functionalists on much, but they also think that one particular Identity is more important than all the others: **Class Identity**. For Marxists, being in the working class (**Proletariat**) is simply the most important thing about you: denying this is **false class consciousness** and waking up to the truth of it is **class consciousness**. Focusing on other Identities like Gender or Ethnicity is a distraction and playing into the hands of the ruling class (**Bourgeoisie**) who want to keep the workers divided.

More recently, **Neo-Marxism** ('New Marxism') has developed, which has a looser understanding of what is meant by the ruling class. This leads to the idea that whole Identities might be 'privileged' or 'oppressed.' People with privileged Identities are engaged in oppression without even realising it. There are privileged Class Identities (being middle-class) but there is also White privilege and male privilege too.

The Marxist thinker **Antonio Gramsci (1891-37)** offered a word that is very useful in this context: **hegemony**. Hegemony is the dominance in society of influential ideas and it can be extended to include the privileged (or '**hegemonic'**) Identities: Whiteness, masculinity, straightness, etc.

CONFLICT PERSPECTIVE: FEMINISM

Traditional Feminism (**1st and 2nd Wave**) focused on women's **Feminine Gender Identity** and the way it is oppressed in **patriarchal society**. These Feminists tended to overlook the distinctive experiences of women from other backgrounds – for example, Black Women were marginalised and the Feminist Movement was led by middle-class women who overlooked working-class women. They tended to adopt the view that, if the laws could be changed to remove discrimination against White middle-class women, all would be right for all women everywhere.

By the 1990s, much legal discrimination against women in the UK and USA had ended thanks to Feminist campaigning, but it was becoming obvious that problems had not gone away, which is why **Crenshaw's Intersectional Theory** became so popular.

Intersectional Feminism represents a **3rd Wave of Feminism** (in the '90s) and with the recognition of trans identities in the 2010s this has become **4th Wave Feminism**. 4th Wave Feminists see the struggle for acceptance of trans women as part of the Feminist struggle, however this has led to conflict within the movement.

Traditional Feminists are concerned that intersectionality leads to specifically *women*'s issues being crowded out by other Identities. 4th Wave Feminism has intensified this concern with the recognition of trans women as women. Feminists who object to this are termed **TERFs (Trans Excluding Radical Feminists)** – but they themselves prefer the term **Gender Critical Feminists**. The disagreement between the two sides is particularly intense and hostile. There is a political side as governments consider allowing people by law to 'self-identify' as a preferred sex, without any medical certification – a policy supported by most Intersectional Feminists but opposed by Gender Critical Feminists.

SOCIAL ACTION PERSPECTIVE: INTERACTIONISM

The Consensus and Conflict Perspectives have something in common: they are **structuralist theories**. Structuralism is the idea that social experience is shaped by structures that are much larger than the individual. Structuralism views society as a powerful set of institutions (the class system, the family, the workplace, religion, etc) that control human behaviour. There is very little possibility for **freewill**. Individuals are not very important in structuralist thinking.

The opposite is a **social action theory** that views individuals has having a lot of **agency** (the power to make changes). According to this view, individuals choose to go along with social institutions, but they also choose to resist them or even replace them. Social action theory views people as capable of rising up against social control and actually altering the powerful institutions, when they choose to.

Structuralist theories are sometimes called **macro action theories** while social action is a **micro action theory** (macro meaning large, micro meaning small).

Social action theories recognise that **culture** and **socialisation** have an effect on people. However, they claim that people can rebel against socialisation and that charismatic and influential individuals can change their surrounding culture. Historical figures like **Martin Luther King Jr** and **Gandhi** serve as examples.

Symbolic Interactionism – or just **Interactionism**, for short – is a social action theory associated with **George Herbert Mead** and **Max Weber**. It views society as **the product of human interactions and the meanings that individuals give to those interactions**. It acknowledges that humans have agency and are not dominated by forces outside their control; humans *create their own meanings*.

Interaction views most things in society as the result of a trade-off or negotiation. For example, your parents **socialise** you to grow up to be a certain sort of person, and you go along with this in some ways but you resist their influence in other ways. Socialisation is never entirely successful but neither is it ever a complete failure. **Culture** is partly something that shapes the way we think and feel, but it's also the result of our thoughts and feelings and humans can change their culture.

You can use the social action perspective or Interactionism to evaluate the ideas in **Chapters 1 and 2** *– see* **Chapter 4** *for more on evaluation (p87).*

Historic Interactionist: Max Weber (1864-1920)

Max Weber (1864-1920) was one of the founding fathers of Sociology (alongside **Karl Marx** p13 and **Emile Durkheim** p11). Weber viewed structural and action perspectives as part of a full understanding of society. He argued that **'Verstehen'** or **empathetic understanding** is crucial to understanding human behaviour. He believed we could make generalisations about human motivations and he thought that social structures encourage certain general types of motivation. Weber argues there are four motivations: (1) **Traditional** involves respecting the past; (2) **Affective** means acting on powerful emotions and not thinking about the consequences; (3) **Value-Rational** means believing in a certain moral code; (4) **Instrumental-Rational** means scientific-style thought which does things to get particular results.

For example, you go to school because you enjoy it (**Affective**) and because you think it would be wrong to truant or skip lessons (**Value-Rational**) and probably because you think the qualifications will help you get a good job (**Instrumental-Rational**) but some people might also come from a religion which tells them they have a duty to get an education (e.g. Hinduism) which is **Traditional**. This shows how a social structure like religion interacts with individual motives.

Contemporary Interactionist: Howard Becker (b. 1928)

Howard Becker developed a type of Interactionism called **Labelling Theory** in his book *Outsiders* **(1963)**. Becker suggests that our interactions with others causes us to pick up 'labels' that affect our other people view us and therefore how future interactions work out. In particular, the **Agencies of Social Control** often judge us by our labels and treat us appropriately. Some people are given **deviant labels** (e.g. 'thief' or 'promiscuous'). Over time, we can **internalise** labels and believe they are part of our Identity: this is the **Self-Fulfilling Prophecy (SFP)**. Some labels have **Master Status** and overrule all other labels. For example, if you have the label 'drug addict' people will judge you badly and ignore your other labels like 'Kind-Hearted' or 'Devoted Daughter.'

For example, if two children fight in the playground, this might be labelled as 'rough play' or as 'thuggish' depending on whether the children are viewed positively or not by their teacher. A child labelled as a 'thug' might internalise the label through SFP and start to see themselves as violent and dangerous.

IDENTITY: A TOOLKIT

Identity is strongly linked to **agencies of socialisation** and it's appropriate to discuss socialisation in exam questions about Identity. For example, Social Class Identity is a product of **primary socialisation by the family**, but also **secondary socialisation in education** and **the workplace** (e.g. **Willis**' study of 'the Lads,' p41).

Similarly, Identity is linked to living within a **Culture** (*c.f.* **Chapter 1**) and Identities are affected by the rise of **Global Culture** (p23) and **Hybrid Cultures** (p26) in particular.

ASPECTS OF IDENTITY: ETHNICITY

Most sociologists reject the idea of 'race' as something non-scientific. Even when it does have some medical value to identify people by race (for example, in identifying relative risks of some genetic disorders like sickle cell disease), race is less important than social factors for determining behaviour.

Ethnicity is a source of identity based on **Culture** and **Socialisation**. Ethnicity is based on language, religion, traditions of dress and food and the belief (whether true or not) that you share ancestors with other people. Ethnic groups are **'imagined communities'** (**Anderson**, **1993**, p71) that exist because people *believe* that they do. Members of ethnic groups may see themselves as culturally distinct from other groups, and are seen, in turn, as different. In this sense, ethnic groups always co-exist with other ethnic groups.

For some people, ethnicity is a very important source of Identity; for others it means little and only becomes important when they get married or during religious festivals.

In the UK, White British is the majority ethnic group (80.5% of the population in the 2011 Census) and other communities are minority ethnic groups (e.g. 3.3% Black, 7.5% Asian). The White British Identity is **hegemonic** (dominant, influential, considered to be the norm) and Neo-Marxists would say it is **privileged** (enjoys benefits and advantages over the other ethnic groups). The term **'White Privilege'** was popularised by **Peggy McIntosh** in *White Privilege: Unpacking the Invisible Knapsack* **(1988)**, an essay which lists the advantages White people enjoy without realising it in American society.

Research: White Privilege: download McIntosh's original (short) essay and learn about the items in the "knapsack"

BAME stands for **Black, Asian & Minority Ethnic**. It's a term the media and UK governments have used for anyone who isn't white British. BAME are often identified by the data as disadvantaged because of discrimination. For example, unemployment rates for BAME people are almost double that for White British and BAME people are overrepresented in UK prisons compared to the average population.

One explanation for this is the idea of **systemic racism** in British society – sometimes it is called **structural racism** or **institutional racism** (**Carmichael & Hamilton, 1967**). This is different from individual racist behaviour; instead, it describes processes at work in institutions like school teaching, businesses hiring and firing, police arrests, courts sentencing and healthcare that disadvantage BAME people. It is not obvious and the people working in these institutions might not be racists themselves, but they end up carrying out practices with racist outcomes (like giving Black boys more detentions or not promoting Asian women).

Functionalists like **Tony Sewell (2021)** argue that, while *individual* racism exists, *systemic* racism does not and Britain is no longer a country where *"the system is deliberately rigged against ethnic minorities."* However, a report from the **Runnymede Trust (2021)** denies this, claiming there is evidence that systemic racism in the UK is getting *worse*.

For **Interactionists**, ethnicity is a **label** with **master status** (p68) that we tend to internalise until a **self-fulfilling prophecy** occurs. **Avtar Brah (2006)** claims young British Asians are skilled **code-switchers** who can change between a British and an Asian Identity (for example, being British with workmates or Asian with family) to gain the benefits of the label at the right place and time.

AO2 ILLUSTRATION: THE WINDRUSH GENERATION

Empire Windrush was a ship that arrived in the UK on 22 June 1948 with 492 passengers: workers from Jamaica, Trinidad and Tobago and other Caribbean Islands and their children. They had come to work in post-War Britain which was experiencing a labour shortage. Many took jobs in the newly-formed NHS or in the transport sector (on trains and in buses). Half a million immigrants from Commonwealth countries arrived in Britain during the 1950s and '60s and those from Caribbean countries were known as the **'Windrush Generation'** after the ship that brought the first families.

Empire Windrush (source: Imperial War Museums)

The Windrush Generation encountered racism and discrimination, but also created a successful place for themselves in British society: Jamaican-born **Sam Beaver King** became the first Black London mayor; actor and comedian **Sir Lenny Henry** is the son of a couple from Jamaica; Labour MP **David Lammy** describes himself as a *"proud son of the Windrush."*

In 2018 there was a scandal when ageing members of the Windrush Generation or their children were threatened with deportation – and 83 people were ***actually deported***. This was exposed as a mistake by the Home Office, which showed "*ignorance and thoughtlessness*" (**Williams, 2020**) in the way it treated the Windrush Generation in Britain.

RESEARCH PROFILE: GILROY (1993)

Winston James (1993) argues that, although the Windrush Generation came from different Caribbean countries with different cultures, their common experience of racism in Britain and being lumped together based on their skin colour caused them to develop a shared Black Identity. In *The Black Atlantic*, historian **Paul Gilroy** (himself a mixed-race child of the Windrush Generation) argues that a new Black Atlantic Identity has developed. This is a type of **Hybrid Culture** (p26) because it is not based on the Caribbean culture of these people's parents or grandparents – in fact, many 2nd or 3rd generation Black British people have little personal connection to the Caribbean. Instead, this new Identity is one shared by Black Americans through things like Rap music and identification with the sufferings of their slave ancestors. Black Atlantic Identity, says Gilroy, is more important than **National Identity**.

The way the US-based **Black Lives Matter Movement** was adopted by Black British protestors in 2020 might be evidence for the existence of this Black Atlantic Identity (since Black British people are not routinely shot or murdered by the police). However, Gilroy has been criticised for ignoring Gender Identity and focusing too much on the masculine Black Atlantic Identity at the expense of women (**Tsitsi Jaji, 2014**)

Research: the Windrush scandal, the 2021 CRED Race Report, Black Lives Matter, Taking the Knee, hip-hop subculture, the Notting Hill Festival, the Black Panthers

ASPECTS OF IDENTITY: NATIONALITY

A **nation** is a country with its own government. National Identity is a sense of belonging to that community and sharing its history. It is often expressed through supporting national sports teams and symbols like flags, holidays and anthems and speaking the national language.

Benedict Anderson (1983) argues that a nation is really an "**imagined community**." A person will never meet most of the people in their nation or visit most of the places in it, so the sense of belonging to a country is in the imagination: in other words, it is **socially constructed**. Anderson thinks that National Identity is a relatively recent thing: it was brought about by '**print Capitalism**' when printing presses started creating books in native languages (instead of Latin) and grew more influential with the development of mass circulation newspapers in the 19th century.

National Identity is important for **Functionalists**: it offers a way for people from very different backgrounds to **share the same values** and experience **social solidarity**. Most Functionalists think the nation is the best political arrangement yet devised to offer people freedom along with security, progress along with a sense of continuity with the past.

Marxists are suspicious of National Identity, since they regard the shared values of nationalism as an illusion created by **ruling class ideology**. They focus instead on how nations go to war and National Identity makes the **working classes** fight each other instead of uniting against their real enemy: the ruling class.

Feminists tend to view National Identity as a distraction from the business of liberating women from oppression. However, it is sometimes supposed that, if there were more women in positions of power, nations would be better led and there would be less war.

For **Interactionists**, nationality is a **label** with **master status** that we tend to internalise until a **self-fulfilling prophecy** occurs. In the 21st century, people have different labels to choose from, such as 'European' or 'Scottish' rather than the traditional 'British.'

AO2 ILLUSTRATION: THE (DIS)UNITED KINGDOM

The **United Kingdom** is made up of several countries. England absorbed Wales through military conquest in the 13th century. However, because of the surviving Welsh language, the Welsh retain a separate sense of Welsh National Identity.

Scotland was always a separate country but England and Scotland unified in 1707 as the Kingdom of Great Britain.

Ireland was added to the United Kingdom of Great Britain in 1801 but became independent in 1922, leaving just the province of Northern Ireland remaining in the United Kingdom.

Because of this unusual history, there are several National Identities in the UK: Welsh, Scottish, Irish and English. There is also a hybrid British Identity that covers all four. **Krishan Kumar (2003)** argues that English Identity has been absorbed by the larger British Identity, leaving the English without a distinct sense of their own Identity.

These tensions emerged in 2014 with the Scottish Independence Referendum, in which Scots voted by 55% to 45% to stay in the UK. The high vote for Scottish independence surprised many people. In 2016, in the EU Referendum, the UK voted by 52% to 48% to leave the EU ('Brexit'). This was an unexpected result and in Scotland the result was 62% for Remain and only 38% for Leave, triggering demands for a second Scottish Independence Referendum.

Some commentators suspect the Brexit vote the result of a strong sense of British National Identity and that the sense of Scottish National Identity lead to the breakup of the UK following a future referendum. Others are concerned that rising National Identity will lead to increasing discrimination against ethnic minorities.

RESEARCH PROFILE: SARDAR (2002)

Ziauddin Sardar suggests that the world is in the middle of a **'global identity crisis.'** Sardar points out that National Identity depends on a sense of 'Other' – a group you are opposed to, some sort of external enemy. The British used to define themselves against their European rivals, the French and the Germans. Americans defined themselves in opposition to Russian Communism during the 'Cold War.' Sardar points out that, after the Cold War ended, American were left uncertain of their identity until the 911 attacks created a new war against terrorism. However, many of these old conflicts have ended so there is a struggle to find a new National Identity: *"When the foundations of our identity crack we lose not only the sense of who we are, but a sense of how we connect to all other identities."*

Sardar agrees with **Functionalists** that a confident sense of Identity is needed and thinks a successful National Identity needs to focus on what we share in common. However, he thinks Identity in the 21st century must also embrace diversity and multiculturalism.

Research: the Brexit referendum, campaigns for independence (e.g. Scotland, Catalonia, Kurdistan), nationalist politics in Europe, the history of the National Anthem or the Union Jack, the Last Night At The Proms

Brexit (photo: Mick Baker)

ASPECTS OF IDENTITY: GENDER

Sex is a biological description and there are two sexes: male and female. **Gender** is a social construct about how to live and behave. Traditionally there are two genders (**masculine** and **feminine**) but people now identify by more genders, such as **nonbinary** (rejecting masculine and feminine being opposites) or **transgender** (identifying with a gender different from sex at birth).

This is a traditional sociological view, but some sociologists propose that gender and possibly sex as well are better understood as a spectrum than a binary. We will consider this later in the course.

Traditional gender roles are for femininity to be passive, emotional, subordinate and decorative (**Talcott Parsons** calls this the **expressive role**, p11) and masculinity to be competitive, unemotional and dominant (the **instrumental role**). Many people now find these gender roles restrictive and even damaging. Women wish to seek independence and not be judged by their appearance while men want to explore their emotional sides. Traditional masculinity is sometimes viewed as **"toxic masculinity"** – related to violence and abusive relationships.

This links to **primary socialisation**, with some couples choosing to raise their children as **'gender neutral'** – not revealing whether the child is a boy or a girl for many years, perhaps until they start school. They hope the child will be happier and healthier without having someone else's expectations of gender imposed on them. It links to **secondary socialisation** with pressure on the Media to represent gender in a more diverse and less stereotyped way.

Conflict Theorists regard traditional Gender Identities as oppressive and welcome the new changes. For example, **Anne Oakley** (p39) explores how socialisation shapes traditional Gender Identities and **Eli Zaretsky** (p36) sees these Identities as helping to support Capitalism.

For **Interactionists**, gender is a **label** with **master status** that we tend to internalise until a **self-fulfilling prophecy** occurs. In the 21st century, people have more power to **negotiate** these labels, creating their own sense of Gender Identity rather than going along with everyone else's.

AO2 ILLUSTRATION: THE LADETTES

Punk subcultures (p53) popularised more aggressive, less conventionally feminine Gender Identity back in the '70s. In the '90s these Identities became more mainstream with the appearance of 'Ladettes': young women who engaged in the sort of behaviour usually associated with young men, such as binge drinking, fighting, using obscene language and seeking out casual sex. Ladette Identity was represented by celebrities like Sarah Cox and Denise Van Outen.

According to **Angela Smith (2013)**: *"The 'ladette' liberated young women from the confines of a very conservative form of femininity because they could behave just like men."* Some people found 'Ladette' subcultures very empowering but there was a backlash in the Media, with sensationalist news stories about out-of-control girls and scare stories about dangerous drinking. By the mid-2000s, the subculture had faded, but Smith argues that it changed our view of femininity for the better: "[Now] *there is a greater acceptance of different gender roles. It's much more acceptable to behave in a diverse way."*

RESEARCH PROFILE: FALUDI (1999)

Susan Faludi is an American **Feminist** whose 1991 book *Backlash: The Undeclared War Against Feminism* is considered a modern Feminist classic. Faludi analyses news stories from the 1980s to show that, as Feminine Identity started to include independence, financial success and career ambitions, there was a backlash, promoting negative stereotypes of career women as bad mothers and marriage-wreckers, spreading myths about an 'infertility epidemic' and successful women who were lonely and unfulfilled without a man. Faludi carries out a content analysis of how women are represented in '80s TV and film and shows a shift towards homemakers, with career women being shown as tragic or monstrous (e.g. the 1987 thriller *Fatal Attraction*).

This is good evidence for the influence of **Patriarchy** and the Media as an **agency of social control** for women (p54). **Peggy Phelan (1993)** criticises Faludi for ignoring working class and Black women in her analysis – an **Intersectionality** criticism (p62)

Faludi's next book was ***Stiffed: The Betrayal of the American Male* (1999)**, in which she argues that, despite Patriarchy, most ordinary men are powerless: underpaid or unemployed, disillusioned with society and often rejected by women. Faludi agrees with sociologists like **Martin Mac An Ghaill (1994)** who detect a **'crisis in masculinity'** because Masculine Identity no longer involves being the provider for the family (the 'breadwinner').

Faludi interviews a **Subculture** (p24) of Los Angeles schoolboys who called themselves the 'Spur Posse' and awarded each other points for having sex with as many young women as possible. They briefly became media celebrities when their deviant behaviour was reported and 9 were arrested, appearing on TV chat shows. The boys were obsessed with being media celebrities and treated their sexual behaviour as a TV gameshow and their gang as a 'brand.' Faludi terms them 'Lost Boys' after the characters in *Peter Pan* (1911) who cannot grow up. Despite their immoral and sexist behaviour (and one went to prison for sexual assault), Faludi presents the boys as tragic and confused people who blame women for their bad luck and social exclusion.

Faludi's study of the Spur Posse is similar to **Willis'** *study of 'the Lads' (p41) – unstructured interviews and observations over a period of time, with the boys being aware that the researcher is a sociologist but still being very open and honest about their deviant attitudes. The boys' relationship with the Mass Media is interesting when we consider* **Postmodernism** *in* **2A***.*

Functionalists would identify the Spur Posse as poorly-socialised and **Marxists** would see them as experiencing **false consciousness** because they mistakenly see women as their enemy rather than the ruling class. For **Feminists** they exemplify **toxic masculinity** – a hostile attitude to women that all men to some extent share but most are better at concealing. For **Interactionists**, the boys are negotiating a deviant label, trying to reinterpret themselves as media heroes and 'winners.'

Research: the film *Fatal Attraction* and its Feminist critique; children raised as gender neutral; examples of Ladette behaviour; examples of toxic masculinity

ASPECTS OF IDENTITY: SOCIAL CLASS

A class is **a group of people who share the same social and economic situation**, normally because they do similar work.

Observing 19th century Britain, **Karl Marx** (p13) identified a vast working class (the **Proletariat**) labouring in the factories of the Industrial Revolution in dangerous and unrewarding conditions, being paid a tiny wage, and a small ruling class (the **Bourgeoisie**) who owned those factories and who creamed off all the profits.

Other sociologists identify a three-tier class system:

- **Working class:** doing manual labour (physically demanding) in low paid jobs

- **Middle class:** doing non-manual labour (often working in offices) in well-paid jobs, often with the help of professional qualifications (e.g. a doctor)

- **Upper class:** not needing to work; they inherit their wealth

According to this view, the upper class promote **High Culture** (p18) and the middle classes imitate them to acquire **cultural capital** (p19).

Marxists tend to regard the middle classes as particularly confused and inauthentic: since they have to work for a wage, they properly belong to the working class, but instead they try to distance themselves from the Proletariat and imitate the culture of the Bourgeoisie – classic **false class consciousness**. **Functionalists** view this system as reflecting **Meritocracy** (p60): education is supposed to give people **social mobility**, enabling working class students to enter the middle class by gaining qualifications.

Marxists like **Antonio Gramsci** have argued that, in order to preserve their power, the ruling class have *shared* some of their privileges, creating a coalition of **hegemonic groups** in society. For example, the super-rich business people or Hollywood A-listers. This **Hegemony** has replaced the old idea of the landed aristocracy and factory owners.

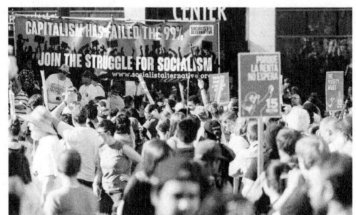

Marxism aims not just to understand society, but to change it (photo: K.G.23)

AO2 ILLUSTRATION: CATEGORISING SOCIAL CLASS

The **Registrar General's Social Class Scale** was used by the UK Government 1911-1980. It groups families into social class based on the occupation of the main earner (traditionally, the man).

Social Class	Examples of occupations
I Professional and managerial	Accountant, doctor
II Intermediate	Teacher, farmer
III Non-manual – skilled occupations	Police officer, secretary
IV Manual – skilled occupations	Electrician, bus driver
V Semi-skilled manual	Bar staff, postal worker
VI Unskilled manual	Cleaner

This scale ignores the unemployed and the independently wealthy (people who don't need to work because they are so rich). **Feminists** objected to the assumption that the man's occupation should determine the social class for the entire family.

A more modern system is the **National Readership Survey (NRS)** scale – also known as the ABC1 system. This scale is used in advertising, market research and journalism. ABC1 are grouped together as middle class and C2DE as working class.

Grade	Social class	Chief income earner's occupation	Frequency (2016)
A	upper middle class	Higher managerial or professional	4%
B	middle middle class	Intermediate managerial, administrative or professional	23%
C1	lower middle class	Supervisory or clerical and junior managerial, administrative or professional	28%
C2	skilled working class	Skilled manual workers	20%
D	working class	Semi-skilled and unskilled manual workers	15%
E	non-working	Casual and lowest grade workers, unemployed on benefits	10%

One problem with the NRS scale is that it doesn't match up to how people see themselves. For example, 45% of the UK population are working class (C2DE) using this system, but the **British Social Attitudes Survey (2016)** found that 60% of British people identify as working class, including many people with middle class (ABC1) jobs.

*It's a common problem with **structuralist** approaches in Sociology that they dictate to people what their identity 'ought' to be. **Interactionists** argue that you have to take people's self-image into account too.*

RESEARCH PROFILE: SAVAGE ET AL. (2013)

This **Great British Class Survey** was carried out in 2011, asking 161,000 adults questions about **economic capital** (wealth), **cultural capital** (p19) and **social capital** (who their friends and contacts were) – based on the ideas of **Pierre Bourdieu (1979)**. Seven social classes were identified:

Elite (6%) - the most privileged group, highest in economic, cultural and social capital; e.g. judges, accountants, doctors.

Established middle class (25%) - the second wealthiest, scoring highly on all three capitals and second highest for cultural capital; e.g. engineers, police constables, midwives.

Technical middle class (6%) - a small new class which is rich but scores low for social and cultural capital (isolated, culturally apathetic); e.g. scientists, business managers.

New affluent workers (15%) - a young class which is socially and culturally active; e.g. sales staff, plumbers, postal workers.

Traditional working class (14%) - scores low on all forms of capital, but is not poor (tends to own houses); e.g. electricians, technicians.

Emergent service workers (19%) - a new, young, urban group which is relatively poor but has high social and cultural capital; e.g. bar staff, nurses, care workers, musicians.

Precariat (**precarious proletariat**, 15%) - the poorest, most deprived class, scoring low for all capitals; e.g. cleaners, shop staff, van drivers.

The survey shows the traditional working class is a shrinking group and no longer the poorest group. Because it includes social and cultural capital, this scale incorporates things beside the job you do and the money you earn.

Research: Discover which class you fit into by taking the test at
https://www.bbc.co.uk/news/special/2013/newsspec_5093/index.stm

ASPECTS OF IDENTITY: SEXUALITY

According to the **Office for National Statistics (ONS)**, in the UK in 2019, 1.4 million people (2.7%) identify as **Lesbian, Gay** or **Bisexual (LGB)**.

In Western cultures, **heterosexuality** is the **norm (heteronormativity)** and some people regard **homosexuality** as deviant. However, views are changing. The **National Survey of Sexual Attitudes and Lifestyles** reveals people became far more tolerant: in 2010, 27% of 16-44 year olds viewed male same-sex relationships as *always or mostly wrong* compared to 60% in 1990. For lesbian relationships, the disapproval was 23% in 2010 compared with 58% in 1990.

In Britain, homosexuality was a crime up until 1967 and the homosexual age of consent only became 16 (the same as heterosexual) in 2001. **Same Sex Marriages** were introduced in 2014. Despite this, LGB people still experience discrimination and violence and 'coming out' as a public Homosexual Identity is stressful for some people.

Many people view sexual orientation as based on biology, claiming you are 'born that way' and that sexual attraction is an instinct. Many sociologists reject this idea and regard sexuality as **socially constructed**: it is learned through **culture** and **socialisation**. For example, **Margaret Mead** (p9) observed the Samoans had a much more open and liberal view of sex than Americans and allowed their young people to experiment with heterosexual and homosexual sex without guilt or anxiety.

Note: saying that Sexual Identity is socially constructed is **not** *the same as saying that sexuality is a choice.*

Functionalists believe that biological needs influence society and tend to view homosexuality as non-functional (because homosexuals do not reproduce) and a possible result of poor **socialisation**. For this reason, functionalists have sometimes supported laws to prevent the 'promotion' of homosexuality in the Media or in Education; e.g. **Clause 28** was such a law (restricting teaching about homosexuality in schools), introduced by Conservative Prime Minister Margaret Thatcher in 1988, but abolished in 2000 in Scotland and 2003 in England & Wales.

Marxists regard **heteronormativity** as something promoted by Capitalism. They argue that, in a non-Capitalist society, people would be free to adopt any Gender or Sexual Identity they liked. Homophobia is based on ruling class ideology, designed to divide the workers and prevent them uniting.

Feminists are even more critical of heteronormativity, because heterosexual relationships are a way for men to oppress women, including sexual violence and domestic abuse. **Radical Feminists** (p15) sometime argue for '**political Lesbianism. Sheila Jeffreys (*Love Your Enemy?*, 1979)** claims that only in same sex relationships can women truly be free from oppression by men: "*all feminists can and should be lesbians.*" However, this assumes that homosexuality is a choice.

AO2 ILLUSTRATION: STONEWALL

In June 1969, police raided the **Stonewall Inn** in New York, which was a popular place for gay people. The customers fought back against the police, led by Black and Hispanic drag queens. The riot and ensuing protests last four days. Protester **Stormé DeLarverie** claimed: "*It was a rebellion, it was an uprising. It wasn't no damn riot*." The event was commemorated a year later with the first Pride March in New York. Groups calling themselves the **Gay Liberation Front** formed and the British GLF organised the first UK Gay Pride Rally in 1972, which became the annual **London Pride** event.

Stonewall Inn, West Village (photo by InSapphoWeTrust)

Peter Tatchell was a member of GLF who went on in 1989 to found the LGB rights charity **Stonewall**, named after the 1969 riots. Stonewall was formed to oppose the government's **Clause 28 legislation**. Stonewall succeeded in this as well as campaigns to equalise the age of consent, end the ban on LGB people in the Armed Forces, win LGB couples the right to adopt children or receive fertility treatment on the NHS and promote awareness and understanding of homosexuality in schools.

In 2015, Stonewall included **Trans rights** in its mission, representing **LGBT** people (rather than just LGB). This has proved controversial and, in 2019, 22 members of Stonewall (including one of the founders, broadcaster **Simon Fanshawe**) formed a breakaway organisation, the **LGB Alliance**. Their argument is that Stonewall now encourages "butch" girls or "feminine" boys to identify as trans, when they are in fact gay. The LGB Alliance has been accused of being transphobic.

RESEARCH PROFILE: McINTOSH (1968)

Mary McIntosh (1936-2013) was a **2nd Wave Feminist** (p15) and **Marxist**. She pioneered the UK lesbian and gay movement (she was a member of the London GLF, *above*). Her 1968 paper *The Homosexual Role* argued that homosexuality was socially constructed at a time when it was treated as a mental illness in Britain and America. She argues that homosexuality exists in all cultures but has different meanings in different times and places. She believes the idea of homosexuality as deviance is in fact a form of **social control**.

McIntosh focuses on the idea of homosexuality as a social role – which is an **Interactionist** view. The role for gay men might include effeminate mannerisms and distinctive preferences in fashion and music. When a man accepts a Gay Identity, he accepts a label and starts to fulfil the expectations of the role (a type of **Self-Fulfilling Prophecy**, p68). McIntosh carried out a survey of men in Leicester and London who had homosexual encounters; married men who saw themselves as 'straight' but admitted being attracted to other men did not act out the homosexual role; gay men who were 'out' did fulfil the homosexual role.

*McIntosh's interviews with homosexual men are considered as part of **2A: Research Methods & Researching Social Inequalities**.*

ASPECTS OF IDENTITY: AGE

Age is an unusual Identity because we *all* experience it and it changes as life goes on: we start out with the Identity of a Child, then Youth, then Adulthood and Middle Age, then Old Age. Sociologists explore this with the idea of **life course**: a process with several stages which change how we see ourselves and how society treats us.

Childhood: Although childhood is a time of **biological maturation**, sociologists recognise that the idea of childhood is **socially constructed**. The age at which you stop being a child varies from culture to culture; for example, 10 is the age of criminal responsibility in the UK, but you cannot be a criminal until you are 15 in Sweden and the age is as low as 6 in some US States (e.g. North Carolina).

Youth (Adolescence): Youth is a stage between Childhood and Adulthood but it seems to be a recent social construction in Western society. In traditional cultures, a child passes into adulthood by completing a rite of passage (e.g. hunting an animal or going through a religious ceremony). In complicated modern societies, a long period of education and training (**Secondary Socialisation**) is needed. Youths have some of the freedoms and responsibilities of adults, but in other ways they are restricted like children.

Adulthood: Cultures also vary over when adulthood begins (the '**age of majority**'). This is 18 in the UK, but 19 in Canada, 20 in Japan and 21 in the US State of Mississippi. **Claire Wallace (1992)** suggests that **cultural 'markers'** signify the beginning of Adult Identity: **private markers** include buying your own clothes whereas **public markers** include moving out of the family home, getting a job or getting married.

Middle Age: Middle Age is difficult to pin down, but it probably begins in the 40s.

Harriet Bradley (1996) claims that in Capitalist societies the Middle-Aged have higher status than the young and elderly because they have the most privileges (e.g. home owners, bosses and managers, political leaders).

There is a **'mid-life crisis' (Elliott Jacques, 1965)** when people become aware of the loss of their youth and the approach of old age and death, leading to anxiety and changes in behaviour (stereotypically, sexual cheating, divorce, gambling, drugs or careless spending).

A symptom of a mid-life crisis is when an ageing man buys a sports car or motorbike to make himself feel youthful (photo: K. Sawyer)

Old Age (Elderly): In traditional societies, the Elderly are respected for their wisdom, but modern Capitalist societies dominated by **Consumer Culture** (p21) view the Elderly as less important. **Orth & Trzesniewski (2010)** suggest that Elderly people in Western societies suffer from negative self-Identity because the society around them values youth, money and work.

Functionalists like **Cumming & Henry** (*Growing Old*, **1961**) propose **Disengagement Theory**: the Elderly need to **'disengage'** from work and political power in order for younger people to take over the roles; disengagement is essential for society to progress. **Marxists** point out that older workers are less productive but claim high salaries, so the Capitalist bosses push them out of the workforce to maintain their profits. **Joung & Miller (2007)** propose **Activity Theory**, which is an **Interactionist** idea that older people benefit both themselves and society if they remain active; they retire from work and identify as Elderly when they perceive ageing to be interfering with their own ability to function.

AO2 ILLUSTRATION: OK BOOMER

The 'Baby Boom' was the big increase in the birth rate in the USA and the UK and other Western countries after the end of World War II. The **'Baby Boomers'** were born between 1946-1965 and are now Elderly or in Middle Age. This generation enjoyed rising standards while it was growing up and a world where work was well-paid, houses were affordable and savings increased in value. The Baby Boomers were the generation that led **2nd Wave Feminism** (p15) and enjoyed the **Popular Culture** of the '60s and '70s, including **Subcultures** like **Punk** (p53).

Laura Gardiner (*Stagnation Generation*, 2016) argues that **Millennials** (born in the 1980s or '90s) will be the first modern generation to be worse off than its parents. Millennials find it harder to buy houses (earning themselves the nickname '**Generation Rent'**) and jobs are less well paid and less secure (with **Zero Hour Contracts** becoming common).

Moreover, because the Boomers are numerous and keen to vote in elections, the power of the '**Grey Vote'** means that politicians must keep the ageing Boomers happy. For example, the UK there is a **"triple lock"** guaranteeing that pensions will keep going up, even when other benefits are being cut. Because the Boomers are likely to live a long time, the Millennials will have to work and pay tax to fund these pensions.

The Boomers have perceptions that the Millennials are selfish and lazy 'snowflakes' who are obsessed with selfies and emotional victimhood. But many Millennials accuse the Boomers of *"stealing the family silver"* i.e. enjoying all the benefits while they were younger and leaving the next generation with economic and environmental problems to clean up.

By the way, the author takes no side in this fight: I'm Gen-X, born in the late '60s-'70s.

RESEARCH PROFILE: ARIÈS (1962), POSTMAN (1994)

French historian **Philippe Ariès** published *Centuries of Childhood* in which he examines the **social construction** of childhood. He argues that in the Middle Ages (10th-13th centuries) *'the idea of childhood did not exist'* and children were viewed as little adults: they were expected to work, they were judged by the same laws as adults and Medieval art shows children wearing the same clothes as adults and joining in all the adult activities, like festivals and prayer. High infant mortality rates encouraged parents not to get too emotionally involved with children who might die; newborn babies often weren't even given names.

Ariès argues that it is only from the 13th century onwards that modern idea of childhood emerged, with childhood being seen as a special time of innocence and children needing to be protected from exposure to things like violence, death or sex.

Neil Postman (*The Disappearance of Childhood*, 1994) developed Ariès' ideas but proposes that Childhood is now disappearing again. Postman argues that mass literacy created a divide between adults who could read and children who would take years to master this skill. However, new technologies like TV and the Internet blur this distinction. Children can quickly learn how to access the 'adult world' so Childhood is disappearing. However, **Sue Palmer (*Toxic Childhood*, 2006)** argues that Childhood has instead become '**toxic'** with too much screen time, less outdoor play and independence, stressful school testing and the targeting of children as consumers through advertising.

Research: Boomers, Gen-X, Millennials or Gen-Z; the influence of the elderly on politics; the 'Grey Pound'; the triple lock on pensions, kidulthood; rites of passage in traditional cultures

ASPECTS OF IDENTITY: DISABILITY

Disability is an unusual Identity because it wasn't recognised as an 'identity' at all until the 1970s. For most of modern history, people have believed in a **medical model of disability**. This sees a disabled person as a normal person with a personal, physical problem that stops them functioning properly.

In the 1970s, the **Union of the Physically Impaired Against Segregation (*UPIAS*, 1975)** claimed: "*In our view it is society which disables physically impaired people.*" **Mike Oliver (1983)** went on to term this the **social model of disability**.

The social model makes a distinction between impairment and disability. **Impairment** is a personal and physical problem. For example, a wheelchair-user has impaired mobility and a deaf person impaired hearing. **Disability** refers to the restrictions imposed by society that exclude people with impairments. For example, not having ramps in buildings disables wheelchair users and not having sign language interpreters disables hearing-impaired people.

This means that the responsibility rests with society to stop impairment from becoming disability. Society is **ableist**: it creates disability then discriminates against it. Some activists think even the term 'disability' is ableist and people with impairments should be termed '**differently abled.'**

Functionalists usually resist the idea that 'society is at fault' for things and tend towards the medical model. However, the 'March of Progress' is an important part of functionalist thinking so they embrace using technology, architecture, etc. to increase access for disabled people, enabling them to contribute to society.

Marxists usually embrace the idea that 'society is at fault' so the social model appeals strongly to them. They see it as a feature of Capitalist society that it disables and excludes people. They claim that in pre-Capitalist societies, communities try to include people with impairments; for example, in Greek mythology the smith of the gods is lame and the poet Homer is blind. However, these ancient societies also practised **infant exposure** (leaving babies to die if they were born with defects).

Feminists like to point out that **Patriarchal** society effectively disables women; lack of access to childcare and maternity provision excludes women from jobs and social life.

Interactionists have a lot to say about Disabled Identities, because society decides what counts as disability and what doesn't and Disability functions as a label with **Master Status** (p68). **The Self-Fulfilling Prophecy (SFP)** means that this label can be internalised and people with disability start to view themselves as inferior or incompetent. **Mary McIntosh**'s idea of the Homosexual Role (p81) applies to disability, because there is also a Disabled Role that people are expected to play in society (being an object of pity, being brave and not complaining, being grateful).

Note that Disabled Identity often intersects with **Age** (because Old Age brings impairments) and **Class** (because disability often makes you poor and socially isolated). Until the 1970s, homosexuality was actually considered to *be* a disability.

AO2 ILLUSTRATION: THE PARALYMPIC GAMES

The **Paralympic Games** have been held since 1960 and allow athletes with disabilities to compete at a world level. The Games have their origin at Stoke Mandeville Hospital in the UK, where wheelchair races were devised for soldiers with spinal injuries. The Paralympics were originally open only to wheelchair-users, but since 1976 other disabilities have been included.

UK Paralympians, such as Jonnie Peacock (sprint runner and amputee), Sarah Storey (swimmer and cyclist with no functioning left hand), David Weir (track and field, wheelchair-user) and Ellie Simmonds (swimmer with genetic dwarfism) are role models for all to admire.

Britain does better at the Paralympics than at the Olympics in terms of medals. Only 25% of countries competing at the Paralympics win gold. This perhaps reflects cultural differences towards disability, with some cultures being more ableist than others.

RESEARCH PROFILE: SHAKESPEARE (2010)

Tom Shakespeare is actually Sir Thomas Shakespeare, 3rd Baronet – a peer of the realm (although he does not use the title) as well as a leading sociologist, a CBE and a wheelchair-user with genetic dwarfism.

Shakespeare offers strengths and weaknesses of the **social model**. He argues that people with disabilities are socialised into seeing themselves as victims, seeing their disability as "*a rationale for their own failure.*" He recognises that the social model is **instrumentally valuable** (it has led to a lot of improvements) and **psychologically valuable** (it removes some of the 'victim mentality' by encouraging people with disabilities to see the problem in society rather than in themselves).

There are problems with forming a positive Disabled Identity. Partly this is because people with disabilities are isolated from each other and lack positive role models (though he himself counts as one).

Shakespeare also argues that the impairment/disability distinction is crude. It's often hard to tell whether a particular problem is due to impairment or socially-imposed disability. Shakespeare suggests that the UPIAS was dominated by wheelchair-users so the social model tends to focus on that sort of disability which can be accommodates with ramps, lifts in buildings, special workstations in offices. The model is less helpful for thinking about learning disabilities, for example.

The social model assumes that all disabled people are, by definition, oppressed. Shakespeare also criticises the ideal of a disability-free society for people with impairments as impractical.

Finally, the social model risks denying that impairment is really a problem by claiming that it's only ableism in society that makes it a problem. But this goes against trying to cure or prevent disabilities. For example, if there's nothing really *wrong* with blindness, why spend money researching cures for blindness?

EXAM PRACTICE: IDENTITY

1. Explain, using examples, the concept of Gender Identity. **[6 marks: 2 AO1 + 4 AO2]**

*This question asks you to give a definition then **two** developed examples. Developed examples will explain why they are examples of the thing you are defining, perhaps using sociological terminology. You should only spend 3 minutes on this question.*

2. Using sources A and B and your wider sociological knowledge, explain the concept of intersecting identities. **[12 marks: 4 AO1 + 8 AO2]**

Source A	Source B
	Intersectionality is the concept that all oppression is linked. Everyone has their own unique experiences of discrimination and we must consider everything that can marginalise people – gender, race, class, sexual orientation, disability, etc. You can always work to be a more intersectional ally by checking your privilege – think about the oppression you don't have to face but others do. Intersectionality is also about learning and understanding other people's experiences. This involves making space for people to tell their own stories and learning from them.

*Write **three** short paragraphs. The first explains the concept ('intersecting identities' in this example). The second paragraph links it to Source A (list the things you see in the picture and explain how they link to the concept). The third paragraph links to Source B using quotes. You could add a fourth point, using an example from your wider knowledge rather than the Sources – but don't overthink this. You should spend 8-10 minutes on this question.*

3. Outline and briefly evaluate the view that age is becoming less important as part of people's Identity. **[20 marks: 8 AO1 + 8 AO2 + 4 AO3]**

*Write **four** paragraphs. The first three paragraphs support the argument in the question (e.g. the global culture is growing in influence) and the fourth argues against it (getting the AO3 marks). For example, you could write about the **Functionalist** idea of older people disengaging from the workforce, then the **Marxist** idea that Capitalism abandons the elderly, then finish off with **Postman's theory of disappearing childhood** (p82) but then argue that age is becoming more important (e.g. the 'Grey Pound'). Allow 20 minutes for this question.*

CHAPTER 4 – EVALUATION

In **Paper 1 Section A**, only question 3 assesses **AO3**/evaluation and the instruction is to *"briefly evaluate"* a viewpoint regarding Culture, Socialisation or Identity.

'Brief evaluation' should be a simple **strength**, **weakness** or **comparison**. As well as the evaluative points you can find in the preceding chapters, here are some evaluative positions candidates can adopt:

"Not all people…" / Over-generalising

Structuralist Perspectives (like **Functionalism** or traditional **Marxism** and **Feminism**) are particularly prone to sweeping generalisations. They often claim that everyone is motivated by the same thing or experiences the same oppression or wants the same outcomes. For example, Functionalists claim everyone shares the same basic values in society and Feminists claim all women are in some way oppressed.

To evaluate these ideas, point out that not all people fit into this mould. Not all Punks are resisting Capitalism (p6), not all housewives are being exploited and enslaved, not all criminals were badly socialised.

If you are writing about some empirical research, point out that its sample group doesn't resemble everyone. Not all delinquent schoolboys are white and working class like 'the Lads' that Paul Willis studied (p41). Even studies with big British or American samples can't be generalised to Europeans or the Chinese.

It's important not to be formulaic. Say *why* not all people are like this: give an example of one of the exceptions. Not all Punks are resisting Capitalism, because some people were only Punks *because they liked the music*. Not all delinquent schoolboys are like Willis' 'Lads' *because some are Black or Asian and they have their own problems with racism*.

"It's out-of-date…" / Time-locked

You will probably have noticed that an awful lot of sociological research comes from the 1950s, '60s and '70s. Those were important decades when a lot of ground-breaking Sociology was done. But do theories and samples from the 1970s tell us anything about the UK in the 21st century?

To evaluate these studies, point out that so much has changed. **Mass employment in factories** has ended, **equal rights for women** has arrived (at least, in principle), the UK has **become a multicultural society**, the **Internet** has transformed the way we communicate and find out about the world (this last point makes studies from the 1980s and early '90s out-of-date too).

Once again, it's important not to be formulaic. Say **why** one of these changes matters for this particular study: give an example of one of the exceptions. Mary McIntosh's research into the Homosexual Role (p81) is out-of-date **because we have same-sex marriages now so gay people can live in the same way as straight people**. Willis' research into 'the Lads' is out-of-date **because 21st century schoolboys don't expect to get a lifelong job in a big factory if they leave school with no qualifications**.

"It's a macro-perspective / Interactionist critique

Structuralist Perspectives make sweeping generalisations because they study society as a whole and focus on important institutions rather than individual people. The **Interactionist** Perspective criticises this, saying it is better to look at society 'from the bottom up' (a **micro Perspective**). The sociologist Max Weber recommends using **Verstehen** – empathic understanding – rather than focusing on big trends.

To evaluate these ideas, point out that an Interactionist approach might be better. Rather than study Punks as a trend in society, take a micro approach and study individual Punks.

As usual, avoid being formulaic. Say **why** the micro approach would be better: give an example of one of the benefits. Take a micro approach to studying Punks, **because they will tell you why they personally are into Punk, which may or may not have anything to do with Capitalism**.

"This is similar to…" / Comparisons

Sometimes, different sociologists or different Perspectives end up saying similar things, although usually for different reasons Marxists and Feminists both agree there is propaganda and brainwashing (**ideology**) in the news and in schools. Marxists and Functionalists both agree that modern Capitalism is stressful and difficult for ordinary people. Interactionists and Marxists both agree that the police treat you badly if you have got certain stigmatised Identities.

To evaluate these ideas, point out the similarity between the sociology you are writing about and another Perspective or research study. If you have explained that Marxists think that nationalism is brainwashing, explain that Interactionists also think National Identity is a label.

As usual, don't be formulaic. Say **why** the two approaches are so similar **or** say why they are also different: give an example. Marxists and Interactionist agree on nationalism because they both think we're under pressure to conform to national stereotypes, **although Marxists think this pressure comes from ruling class ideology** and **Interactionists focus more on how national labels have master status** (p68).

"Nature rather than nurture…" / The Nature-Nurture Debate

Sociologists tend to assume that everything is socially constructed, but it's worth remembering that biology might be playing a neglected role in human behaviour.

To evaluate these ideas, point out that a Nativist approach might be better. Rather than explain gender roles through social control, maybe there are innate biological differences.

It would be formulaic just to say "maybe there are innate biological differences" and leave it at that. Say *why* the Nativist approach would be better: give an example of one of the benefits. Take a Nativist approach to studying gender roles, *because it might tell you why men and women tend to behave differently in lots of cultures, e.g. male aggression*.

"An Intersectionalist would say …" / Intersectional critique

Intersectional sociology (p63) tends to be from a Neo-Marxist or Feminist Perspective, but it makes a powerful criticism of even traditional types of Marxism and Feminism.

Intersectionality identifies a 'grid of oppression' in society that doesn't always match up with traditional Sociology. For example, traditional Marxists see the working class as oppressed, but Intersectionalists point out that the White working class males have **privileges** based on ethnicity and gender. There are also privileges based on cis (as opposed to trans) gender and ableism that are ignored by traditional Conflict Theorists.

In order to avoid being formulaic, say *why* an Intersectional approach would be better: give an example of the benefits. Take an Intersectional approach to studying the Elderly, *because it will reveal the particular difficulties Black or Gay older people that White, heterosexual people don't*.

"A weakness of this Perspective is …" / Standard theoretical critiques

Functionalism

Functionalism ignores diversity: Functionalism assumes we are all the same and want the same things, but the things it says we all want tend to be the sort of things that the white middle classes want. Functionalism doesn't take seriously the idea that ethnic minorities, the working class or women might have different goals and values.

Functionalism ignores social injustice: Functionalism assumes that society is harmonious and **meritocratic** (p60) but it turns a blind eye to a lot of inequality, corruption and barriers to social mobility. It assumes that racism, sexism, etc. are '*in the past*' and there isn't a need to reform society in a major way. It defends Capitalism as the best system we have discovered for making people healthy and wealthy while ignoring the huge human and environmental cost of Capitalism worldwide.

Functionalism celebrates Western superiority: Functionalists believe in the **'March of Progress'** (p10) and claim that the sort of liberal democratic nations you find in Europe, North America and Australia are the most advanced. Other societies ought to imitate them and immigrants ought to fit in. This ignores many flaws in Western societies (e.g. the slave trade, dropping nuclear bombs, abuse of women, ruining the environment) which Marxists and Feminists point out.

Functionalism overrates the biological: Functionalists believe society reflects unchangeable biological needs or 'human nature.' Critics argue there is no such thing as 'human nature' and that everything is **socially constructed**. 'Human nature' is often used to excuse arrangements that are blatantly sexist or racist or homophobic.

Marxism

Marxism ignores progress: In the last 200 years, Capitalist societies have abolished slavery, set up human rights, created a welfare state and free education and healthcare for all. Marxists often talk as if this hasn't happened or as if it happened *in spite of* Capitalism. This pessimistic view of the past and the future perhaps exaggerates social injustice as much as Functionalism downplays it.

Marxism is a conspiracy theory: It's standard for Marxists to argue that the Media (especially the news), Education and the Workplace are all controlled by a sinister group of billionaires who brainwash everyone through **ideology**. This underestimates the independence of many journalists, teachers and bosses as well as the ability of ordinary people to think for themselves and work out what's true.

Marxists assume class is homogenous: *Homogenous* means 'all the same' and traditional Marxists think that all working class people share the same relationship to labour and power. **The Great British Class Survey** (p78) shows how much class has changed. Marxism underestimates the diversity in the working classes and this leads to Marxists ignoring Ethnic, Gender and National Identities among others. However, **Neo-Marxists** (p66) are more aware of **intersecting Identities**.

Marxism offers no solutions: You don't have to be a Marxist to spot the Capitalism has flaws – Functionalists would admit *that*! Marxists argue that Capitalism is intrinsically rotten and destructive and it needs to be replaced rather than reformed. But replaced with what? Communism has been tried by many countries in the last century but the results don't suggest it is any better at removing poverty and protecting human rights – in fact, it might be much worse. Marxism can be accused of criticising Capitalism without offering a coherent alternative.

Feminism

Feminism ignores biology: Feminists insist that gender is **socially constructed,** and it certainly is up to a point. However, Psychology reveals lots of biological differences in brain structure, hormones and genes between the sexes and it's unlikely that *none* of this makes *any* difference to social behaviour. But if Gender Identity is even partly based on unchangeable sexual differences, then some of the situations women are in might not be *entirely* due to Patriarchy.

Feminism ignores progress: In the last century women have won the vote, the right to be educated at university and manage their own affairs. In Britain, the law has been changed to allow abortion and divorce, freeing women from inequitable relationships, and legislation starting with the Sexual Discrimination Act (1975) has outlawed sexual discrimination. Feminism can be accused of downplaying this progress and exaggerating the scale of injustice. **Intersectional Feminism** (p67) is a response to this criticism that 'feminism's job is done.'

Feminists assume gender is homogenous: As with Marxists and social class, traditional Feminists are accused of treating all women as if they experienced the same oppression – which in practice means assuming that the difficulties of White women are typical for all women. Clearly, Black women and Lesbian women have different experiences and **Intersectional Feminism** has come about through an attempt to recognise this.

Feminists ignore the oppression of men: Feminists sometimes seem to assume that Masculinity is homogenous and all men are complicit in the Patriarchy, but men are much more likely than women to die by violence, to be victims of crime and to work in dangerous conditions. Many men are also victims of oppression. **Intersectional Feminism** recognises this and Feminists like **Susan Faludi** (p75) recognise the **'crisis in masculinity'** as a problem for men as well as women.

Interactionism

Interactionism cannot be generalised: Because it tends to do research on small groups, studying micro relationships and beliefs, it's hard to generalise the conclusions of Interactionism to other groups or society on a macro level.

Interactionism cannot be objective: The close-up and personal nature of Interactionist research and its focus on *Verstehen* (p68) makes it very **subjective** – just a matter of opinion – whereas Sociology claims to be a social *science* that explores facts in an **objective** way.

Interactionism is an incomplete explanation: Even when Interaction identifies processes that seem to be quite generalisable – like the **Self-Fulfilling Prophecy** (p68) – its small-scale micro view means it doesn't explore where these processes come from. Marxists argue that Interactionism is incomplete as an explanation without including Capitalism and **ruling class ideology**. Functionalists would also say Interactionism needs to explain how the experiences of little groups fit into a theory of society's functions and requirements.

EXAM PRACTICE: SECTION A

1. Explain, using examples, the concept of informal social control. **[6 marks: 2 AO1 + 4 AO2]**

*This question asks you to give a definition then **two** developed examples. Developed examples will explain why they are examples of the thing you are defining, perhaps using sociological terminology. You should only spend 3 minutes on this question.*

2. Using sources A and B and your wider sociological knowledge, explain the concept of cultural diversity. **[12 marks: 4 AO1 + 8 AO2]**

Source A	Source B
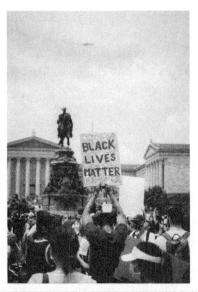	Whether at work, school, or simply out on the town, we're going to meet people from various cultural and ethnic backgrounds, all of whom have different perspectives on the world than our own. People have a tendency to look at someone from a different background and judge them based on negative stereotypes, and that's something we want to push back against and dispel. Instead of staying stuck in our ways, we can learn from one another and respect how someone else lives, even if it's different from our own. Many of the global challenges we face are complex issues, and putting our heads together will only benefit us all in the end.

*Write **three** short paragraphs. The first explains the concept ('diversity' in this example). The second paragraph links it to Source A (list the things you see in the picture and explain how they link to the concept). The third paragraph links to Source B using quotes. You could add a fourth point, using an example from your wider knowledge rather than the Sources – but don't overthink this. You should spend 8-10 minutes on this question.*

3. Outline and briefly evaluate the view that sexuality is becoming more important as part of people's Identity. **[20 marks: 8 AO1 + 8 AO2 + 4 AO3]**

*Write **four** paragraphs. The first three paragraphs support the argument in the question (e.g. the global culture is growing in influence) and the fourth argues against it (getting the AO3 marks). For example, you could write about the idea that sexuality is socially constructed, research suggesting society is becoming more tolerant and accepting and finish off with **McIntosh's study of the Homosexual Role** (p81) but then argue for the opposite (for example, that intersectionality is a more influential idea today). Allow 20 minutes for this question.*

KEY RESEARCH

The 34 studies here over all the topics that arise in **Section A** of the exam and they will prove just as useful in later sections too. Start learning them. For each study, I include the key terms, a Perspective (if relevant) and the particular topics it is linked to.

Althusser (1970): RSA and ISA; **Marxism**; police/military as social control, informal social control, pp37, 51

Back (1996): cultural masks; hybrid culture, global culture, hybrid identity, ethnic identity, p27

Baudrillard (1970): postmodernity, hyper-reality, simulacrum; **Postmodernism**; consumer culture, hybrid culture, hybrid identity, p22

Becker (1963): *Outsiders*, labelling theory, master status, SFP; **Interactionism**; socialisation, social control, identity, p68

Bourdieu (1984): *Distinction*, cultural capital, habitus; **Marxism**; high culture, socialisation, class, p19

Bowles & Gintis (1976): *Schooling in Capitalist America*, hidden curriculum, correspondence principle; **Marxism**; socialisation, education as social control, p45

Colapinto (1998): case of David Reimer; socialisation, gender identity, p32

Crenshaw (1991): intersectionality; **Feminism**; identity, p65

Davis & Moore (1945): meritocracy, stratification; **Functionalism**; education as social control, p60

Durkheim (1912): anomie, social solidarity, social integration; **Functionalism**; socialisation, religion as social control, p11, 58

Faludi (1999): backlash against feminism, Spur Posse; **Feminist**; subculture, socialisation, media as social control, gender identity, p75

Giddens (1999): *Runaway World*, de-traditionalisation, global outlook, cosmopolitanism, reverse colonisation; **Postmodernism**; global culture, hybrid culture, hybrid identity, national identity, ethnic identity, p24

Gilroy (1993): *The Black Atlantic*; hybrid culture, hybrid identity, ethnic identity, p71

Hebdige (1979): Punks, bricolage, CCCS; **Marxism**; subcultures as social control, p53

Malinowski (1964): Trobriand islanders, rites of passage; socialisation, religion as social control, p44

Marx (1844): alienation, proletariat, bourgeoisie, false class consciousness, ruling class ideology; **Marxism**; socialisation, workplace as social control, class identity, pp13, 46

McIntosh (1968): *The Homosexual Role;* **Feminism & Interactionism;** sexual identity, social control, p81

Mead (1928): *Coming of Age in Samoa;* childhood, sexuality, socialisation, social control, cultural diversity, pp9, 32

Mead (1935): *Sex & Temperament in Three Primitive Societies;* gender roles among the Tchambuli; gender, socialisation, cultural diversity, p9

Miliband (1973): media spreads ruling class ideology; **Marxism;** media as social control, p55

Murray (1984): underclass; **New Right;** workplace as social control, class identity, p57

Nayak (2003): white wannabes; hybrid culture, global culture, hybrid identity, ethnic identity, p27

Oakley (1982): canalisation, manipulation, verbal appellation; **Feminism;** socialisation, gender, pp15, 39

Parsons (1959): instrumental & expressive roles, particularistic vs universalistic values; **Functionalism;** gender, socialisation, family & education as social control, pp11, 35, 37, 44, 52

Postman (1994): *The Disappearance of Childhood;* **Postmodernism;** age identity, 83

Sardar (2002): global identity crisis; **Postmodernism;** global culture, national identity, 73

Savage et al. (2013): *Great British Class Survey,* precariat, cultural & social capital; class identity, 78

Shakespeare (2010): social model of disability, intrinsic & psychological value; disabled identity, p85

Storey (2006): 6 types of pop culture; popular culture, consumer culture, 20

Sutherland (1949): white collar crime; law as social control, 49

Thornton (1995): *Club Cultures,* subcultural capital; **Feminism, Postmodernism;** subcultures, age (youth) identity, 25

Willis (1977): *Learning to Labour,* the Lads; **Marxism;** subculture, socialisation, peer group & education as social control, class identity, 41

Wilson & Kelling (1982): broken windows theory, zero-tolerance policing; **Functionalism;** police as social control, p48

Young (1984): social bulimia; **Marxism;** consumer culture, socialisation, media, pp13, 42

FURTHER RESEARCH

These studies are less central to any argument. Some of them just reference a useful piece of terminology. Others offer criticism of a Key Study or are the original research that a Key Study is criticising.

Ahmed (2011): feminist who supports Muslim veil, p43

Anderson (1983): nation as *"imagined community,"* p71

Aries (1962): social construction of childhood, p83

Bradley (1996): privileges for the middle-aged, p82

Brah (2006): Asian code-switchers, p70

Carmichael & Hamilton (1967): systemic racism, p70

Cohen (1955): status frustration, p40

Cummings & Henry (1961): disengagement theory, p82

Davis (2008): critiques **Intersectional Feminism**, p65

Duncombe and Marsden (1995): double shift, p52

Freeman (1983): criticises Mead (1928) p9

Gewertz (1981): criticises Mead (1935) p9

Gramsci (--): introduces idea of hegemonic control to **Neo-Marxism**, p66

Heidensohn (1985): double jeopardy, p49

Jacques (1965): the mid-life crisis, p82

Jaji (2014): criticises Gilroy (1993) p71

Jeffreys (1979): political lesbianism, p79

Joung & Miller (2007): activity theory, p82

Kumar (2003): English identity, p72

Mac An Ghaill (1994): crisis in masculinity, p75

McIntosh (1988): white privilege (Peggy McIntosh, not Mary McIntosh), p69

Money (1975): criticised by Colapinto (1998) p32

Oliver (1983): social model of disability, p84

Orth & Trzesniewski (2010): negative self-image in old age, p82

Palmer (2006): toxic childhood, p83

Phelan (1993): criticises Faludi, p75

Reich (2020): supports defunding the police, p47

Sewell (2021): criticises systemic racism, p70

Smith (2013): critiques Ladettes, p74

Tibi (1998): *Leitkultur*, p17

Wallace (1992): cultural markers in the life course, p81

Weber (--): inspired **Interactionism**, recommended *Verstehen*, p68

Zaretsky (1976): criticises Parsons on family from Marxist Perspective, p36

SECTION B (OPTION 2): YOUTH SUBCULTURES

What's this topic about?

This introduces you to the main sociological theories about Youth, in particular why YOUTH SUBCULTURES form and the appeal of DEVIANT SUBCULTURES for the young.

This should help you answer some important questions:

- What is Youth in society: is it a good thing or a period of stress and danger? Is youth culture significant in society or are young people exploited and marginalised?

- Why is there youth deviance: is it natural for young people to break the rules or are they vulnerable to dangerous pressures? Is society growing more dangerous for the young or are they too coddled from reality?

- What role does the Media play in the lives of young people: is it empowering them, corrupting them or misrepresenting them?

Youth

Like other animals, humans experience biological MATURATION. They mature into adults, gaining size, strength and physical and mental skills but also reproductive characteristics. Puberty is particularly important as a visible indicator of maturation, although maturation continues through the teens and into adulthood.

In many traditional societies, the transition from child to adult is marked by a **rite of passage**, which is usually a religious ceremony and might be accompanied by a test (such as, to hunt an animal). After that, the former child is considered an adult.

'Youth' is an alternative to the institution of a rite of passage. The young person has some adult privileges (staying out late, buying their own clothes, not requiring supervision at all times) but in other ways is still in a childlike state (prevented from joining in many adult activities, like drinking alcohol, working full time or engaging in sex). Youth is a period of training and preparation for adult life.

Because Youth isn't fixed by biology, it is **socially constructed**. Different cultures view Youth starting or ending at different times. For example, you are not considered **criminally responsible** until you are 15 in Sweden, but 6 in North Carolina, USA. The **'age of majority'** (when you are legally allowed to participate in adult activities) is 18 in the UK, but 20 in Japan and 21 in Mississippi, USA.

People have different views on Youth. Some wish to see the age extended, arguing that young people are still not mature enough at 18 or even 21 to handle society's many demands. Others wish to remove it, arguing that young people are being denied their rights and freedoms – for example, to vote on matters that concern them.

CHAPTER FIVE – YOUTH CULTURE

Culture means the things that are shared by a group that mark it out as distinctive. For most of history and in most societies, there was no such thing as 'Youth Culture' because young people weren't a distinctive group. At the start of the 19th century, children started work in factories or in mines at age 10 and joined the Navy at age 12. In other words, as soon as children could function as adults, they did so, and took part in the adult working culture.

As the Industrial Revolution progressed, the idea of children working in dangerous conditions became distasteful to Victorians. UK laws made it compulsory to stay in school till 10, then until 12. At the end of the Second World War, in 1946, the UK school leaving age was raised to 15. Today, it is 18.

Most historians trace the emergence of a distinctive **Youth Culture** to the 1950s and '60s, when young people were not allowed to join the adult world of work but had enough money and independence to interact in society away from home. This Youth Culture expressed itself in distinctive youth fashions and enjoyment of new 'pop' music, new dancing styles and new leisure pastimes.

Right from the beginning, there was a concern that Youth was a period of *'Sturm und Drang'* (*'storm & stress'* according to **G. Stanley Hall, 1904)** where hormones produced out-of-control behaviour. This biological view of Youth takes the Nature side in the **Nature-Nurture Debate**.

Research: the pop music of the 1950s, especially rock & roll (and Elvis Presley!) but also skiffle and jazz; the youth fashions of the '50s in hair and dress; the significance of motor bikes and scooters; the rise of vinyl LPs and the pop charts; pirate radio; dance halls; movies aimed at young people (especially horror, science fiction); boys and girls comics of the '50s and '60s

Elvis Presley defined Youth Culture in the 1950s

Positive Views of Youth Culture

Youth Culture is often praised for its novelty, energy and creativity. Youth Culture generates new fashions, new language in the form of youth slang, new art and new ideas. It often leads the way in protesting injustice and demanding a better future. Whether it's the music of the Beatles or the environmental idealism of Greta Thunberg, new ideas from Youth Culture move into the mainstream culture and change it for the better. It helps society progress.

Youth Culture also benefits young people themselves. Life in 21st century societies is complicated and important decisions have to be made about relationships, lifestyles and careers. Are you straight or gay? Do you take recreational drugs? Do you want to go to university? It's difficult to un-do many of these decisions later and the consequences can be far-reaching. Youth Culture offers a period of experimentation when adolescents can 'try out' some options, make mistakes, break the rules and then 'put it behind them' and move forward.

Negative Views of Youth Culture

Traditionally, Youth Culture was viewed as *'Sturm und Drang'* and linked to out-of-control hormones.

Youth Culture isn't always fresh and spontaneous. It's also a type of **Consumer** and young people are a target for big corporations wanting to sell them things: high sugar sweets and snacks packed with additives, violent video games, music glamorising crime, porn. Youth Culture is **exploitational** and often carries very bad messages about lifestyle and morals.

Similarly, Youth Culture doesn't benefit society as a whole if young people are being **socialised** into a selfish mindset that only cares about appearances and pleasure.

Some worry that Youth Culture is reaching younger children, introducing them to sexual content, bad language and normalising drug-taking or violence when they're too young to understand it properly. Others worry that Youth Culture is extending later into life, so that young people don't 'grow out of it' in their 20s or 30s. This leads to **'Kidults'** who are grown men and women still chasing a lifestyle of drugs, video games and casual sex when they ought to be settling down with families and careers.

RESEARCH PROFILE: MEAD (1928)

Margaret Mead (1901-1978) visited Samoa in the 1920s. Samoa is an island group in the Pacific and, in the early 20th century, the inhabitants had little contact with the outside world. Mead described her findings in *Coming of Age in Samoa* (1928) after studying 68 girls (aged 9-20) from three villages on the island of Ta'ū., especially the village of Fitiuta. Mead learned the Samoan language and used a sociological method called ethnography to observe and record the behaviour of the Samoan girls.

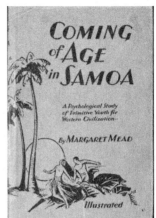

Mead's research challenges the idea that adolescence is necessarily a period of **Sturm und Drang** ('Storm and Stress') because of the biological changes occurring around puberty. Against this strongly Nature-view, Mead argues for a **social constructivist** view that the Samoan girls made the transition to adulthood without 'storm & stress' for three reasons:

Diffusion of responsibility: Children were raised by the whole community rather than just the two parents. This reduced the need for adolescents to rebel against their parents.

Openness: Children were not shielded from death, sex or suffering. Mead describes children watching childbirth happen, including miscarriages.

Sexual freedom: Adolescents were allowed to experiment with sex, including masturbation and homosexuality, without being judged or stigmatised

Mead argues that American culture at that time was confusing and oppressive compared to the carefree culture of Samoa. Mead complains about the conflicting messages American adolescents receive: *"our children are faced with half a dozen standards of morality: a double sex standard for men and women."*

Mead's research was from before the emergence of Youth Culture in the 1950s. Perhaps of Western culture had been more like Samoa, there wouldn't have been as much of a need for Youth Culture in the first place.

Mead's research was criticised by **Derek Freeman (1983)** who lived in Samoa in the 1950s claimed Mead had exaggerated her picture of the guilt-free Samoan adolescence. He interviewed some of the Samoan girls and they denied their promiscuous behaviour, saying they had lied to Margaret Mead.

However, it is possible that contact with the outside world made the Samoans change their behaviour after Mead studied them (for example, they had converted to Christianity). Freeman was interviewing the Samoan girls now they were old women and perhaps felt embarrassed to admit their youthful behaviour.

*Mead's research is an excellent starting point for any essay on Youth Culture. Her **ethnographic approach** will feature in **2A: Research Methods & Researching Social Inequalities**.*

PERSPECTIVES ON YOUTH CULTURE

Perspectives are different ways of interpreting the social world. The four perspectives in this chapter are the ones introduced in **Section A** but another perspective (**Postmodernism**) is added and a sixth (**New Right**) will be introduced in **Chapter 7**.

Perspectives are very broad viewpoints. Individual sociologists from the same perspectives might disagree with each other. Some sociologists straddle more than one perspective. I will take a neutral view on which perspective is "right" or "wrong" and focus instead on how they differ and the ways in which they criticise each other.

CONSENSUS PERSPECTIVE: FUNCTIONALISM

Functionalism starts with the idea of a basic biological component to human social behaviour. This means that societies can be good or bad, based on how successfully that match our biological needs. Societies that go against our biological needs will be **dysfunctional** and throw up problems like unhappiness, crime and self-destructive behaviour.

Emile Durkheim, the founding figure of Functionalism, proposed that modern Capitalism was particularly difficult for people to make sense of, creating **anomie**, which is a state of disconnection from society that ultimately leads to suicide. Social institutions like the family have a function of reducing anomie by promoting **social integration** (a feeling of 'belonging').

Sharing a culture creates a **value consensus** – an agreed sense of how things should be done, what's important, the boundaries of acceptable behaviour and the things to be strived after.

Functionalists claim institutions have a **manifest** (obvious) **function** – something they do that benefits society. However, they also propose that institutions can have a **latent** (hidden) **function** – benefiting society in non-obvious ways.

Youth Culture is therefore a response to Capitalism and perhaps the weakening of institutions like religion. It promotes a sense of belonging (to a peer group) and gives young people a **set of values** to share. In particular, these values emphasise **freedom and transgression** (rules-breaking) to a greater degree than mainstream society. Functionalism buys into the '**Sturm und Drang**' view of Youth (p97) and identifies the **latent function** of allowing young people to 'let of steam' and vent frustrations in a safe way.

When Youth ends, young adults abandon Youth Culture as a 'phase' and adopt the values of mainstream culture. They look back on the transgressive things they did as youths with a mixture of embarrassment and nostalgia.

Of course, there are limits to transgression so Youth Culture cannot be allowed to get too out-of-hand. This is why **agencies of social control** are needed to establish the boundaries of what is acceptable even within Youth Culture.

Research: Go back over your notes on **Section A** and review **Peer Groups** (p40) and **Age Identity** (p81) as well as the ideas of **Durkheim (1912**, p58**)**, **Parsons (1959**, p35**)** and **Davis & Moore (1945**, p60**)**, applying them to Youth Culture

CONFLICT PERSPECTIVE: MARXISM

Conflict is the opposite of consensus and **Marxists** reject the idea that society reflects human biological needs. Marxists believe that **society is shaped by conflict** between a **ruling class** that holds the wealth and power in society and a **working class** that is much more numerous but poor and powerless. For them, there are good and bad societies, with 'good' meaning 'giving power to the working classes' and 'bad' meaning 'allowing the ruling classes to hold all the power.'

For Marxists, Capitalism is not just complicated and stressful to live under, but outright unfair and oppressive. They reject the idea of value consensus because they think the rulers and the workers want very different things. **Ideology** is a set of beliefs that hides and justifies the unfairness in Capitalist society.

Youth Culture is therefore a response to Capitalism. However, while Functionalists see it as a sort of coping mechanism, Marxists see it either as **exploitation** or as **resistance**. Resistance falls short of being outright revolution, but it's still a refusal to join in the behaviour that Capitalism demands and a rejection of the **ruling class ideology** that justifies Capitalism.

Much of Youth Culture is exploitation: young people are being brainwashed into being obedient consumers and workers. They are being trained to value fashions and brands, to care about money and shopping, to value 'fitting in' and 'being popular' and to stigmatise genuine rebels as 'weirdos' and 'freaks.'

However, some **Youth Subcultures** (*c.f.* **Chapter 6**) actively resist Capitalism and show contempt for mainstream society and mainstream Youth Culture. Marxists see this response as much more authentic and valuable. These young people see the truth about society, if only for a short time.

Research: Go back over your notes on **Section A** and review **Peer Groups** (p40) and **Age Identity** (p81) as well as the ideas of **Bowles & Gintis (***Schooling In Capitalist America***, 1976**, p45**)**, **Hebdige (1979**, p53**)**, **Marx (1844**, p46**)** and **Willis (***Learning To Labour***, 1977**, p41**)**, applying them to Youth Culture

CONFLICT PERSPECTIVE: FEMINISM

Feminists argue that **gender** is a significant source of conflict in society. Feminists reject the idea that society's gender roles reflect human biological needs and argue that **society is structured in favour of the interests of males (patriarchy)**: although they make up half the population, women are subordinated to men, they are 'second class citizens' and are threatened with physical or sexual violence to keep them in line. Feminists reject the idea of value consensus because they think males and the females want very different things. They often make use of the Marxist concept of **ideology** – a set of beliefs that hides and justifies the patriarchy, persuading people to ignore or accept sexual discrimination as 'the way it has to be.'

Feminists take a similar view of Youth Culture, that it usually **exploits** young women but it can sometimes express **resistance** to patriarchy.

Youth Culture exploits young women by socialising them into accepting their subordinate roles: girls are encouraged to focus on personal beauty and popularity, acquiring boyfriends and accepting their status as **sex objects**. Girls who do not except this **heteronormative role** (i.e. a role that makes ordinary heterosexuality the rule) are **stigmatised**, often by teasing or bullying or rejection by peers.

However, some Youth Subcultures actively resist patriarchy, encouraging girls to support one another against sexism and encouraging **gender nonconformity**. Many Feminists see the increasing acceptance of nonbinary gender, lesbianism and transsexuality within Youth Culture as a positive thing rather than a cause for alarm.

> **Research:** Go back over your notes on **Section A** and review **Peer Groups** (p40), **Intersectional Identity** (p63) and **Age/Gender Identity** (p81, p74) as well as the ideas of **Oakley (1982**, p39), **Faludi** (*Stiffed*, 1999, p75) and **Crenshaw** (*Mapping The Margins*, **1991**, p65), applying them to Youth Culture

SOCIAL ACTION PERSPECTIVE: INTERACTIONISM

The Consensus and Conflict Perspectives have something in common: they are **structuralist theories** and view society as a powerful set of institutions (the class system, the family, the workplace, religion, etc) that control human behaviour. There is very little possibility for **freewill**. Individuals are not very important in structuralist thinking.

The opposite is a **social action theory** that views individuals as having a lot of **agency** (the power to make changes). Social action theory views people as capable of resisting social control and altering the powerful institutions, when they choose to.

Structuralist theories are sometimes called **macro action theories** while social action is a **micro action theory** (macro meaning large, micro meaning small).

Symbolic Interactionism – or just **Interactionism**, for short – is a social action theory associated with **George Herbert Mead** and **Max Weber**. It views society as **the product of human interactions and the meanings that individuals give to those interactions**. It acknowledges that humans *create their own meanings*.

Youth Culture is partly something that shapes the way young people think and feel, but it's also the result of their thoughts and feelings. Young people can change Youth Culture. This goes against the idea that Youth Culture automatically exploits people or resists Capitalism. It *can* do those things, but it doesn't *have* to. It also goes against the idea that Youth Culture is just a phase young people go through: it *can* be that but it doesn't *have* to be.

Interactionists often use **Labelling Theory (Becker, *Outsiders*, 1963)** to explain how young people are labelled by society (e.g. as troublemakers, as irresponsible) and treated in accordance with those labels; if young people **internalise** those labels then a **Self-Fulfilling Prophecy (SFP)** can occur. Society can make stereotypes about young people come true through labelling. However, young people can negotiate those labels, redefining them. For example, society labels young people as 'lazy' but youngsters can respond by interpreting this as being 'cool' (not showing great concern or hurry over things) and viewing that as a positive thing.

> **Research:** Go back over your notes on **Section A** and review **Intersectional Identity** (p63) and **Age Identity** (p81) as well as the ideas of **Becker** (p68) mentioned above, applying them to Youth Culture

POSTMODERN PERSPECTIVE: POSTMODERNISM

The Perspectives you have studied so far fit together in a sort of pattern. Functionalism (Consensus) is opposed by Marxism/Feminism (Conflict); all three are Structuralist views that are opposed by Interactionism (Social Action).

With Postmodernism, we have a completely different approach. It is sometimes called **'Post-Structuralism'** because instead of structures it emphasises **fragmentation** (things breaking apart) and **fluidity** (things changing into other things). Like Interactionism, it emphasises **choice** but it also draws attention to the **risk** and **uncertainty** that such choice involves.

Postmodernism is best understood as a set of linked ideas about society today:

After Modernity: We tend to use 'modern' to mean 'as things are now' but in Sociology it's a more specific term: a **modernity** is a society that develops science, industrialisation, national government, secularism (religion separated from public life) and individualism. You might think our society is *still like that*, but Postmodernists argue we have moved onto a new phase called **postmodernity** (meaning 'after modernity').

Young people in the 21st century have lived all their lives in postmodernity, creating a big generational divide with their parents who grew up in the 1980s or '90s (i.e. during modernity).

Media Saturation: The Mass Media, particularly the Internet, has invaded people's lives to a degree that the media shapes how people perceive the world. **Baudrillard (1970**, p22) calls this chaotic, exciting but empty way of living **Hyper Reality**.

Young people in the 21st century are raised with access to tablets, digital TV channels and the Internet and experience Hyper Reality most strongly. **Faludi (*Stiffed*, 1999**, p75) describes the Spur Posse, a gang of young men who were obsessed with being TV celebrities and who treated sexual assault like a TV game show.

Diversity, Choice & Fragmentation: Postmodern society is **multicultural** (p17) and affected by **Global Culture** (p23). This means people living in postmodernity have an incredible **diversity** of **choices** available to them: religion (or lack of it), ethics, lifestyle, career, family, education; in fact, their **Identity**. This leads to **fragmentation** as the institutions that used to connect people break down, such as national governments losing authority, borders ceasing to matter, families becoming separated, beliefs becoming more individualistic.

These choices and the risk (see below) that goes with them press particularly on young people.

Fluidity, Risk & Uncertainty: In this fragmented society, choice becomes overwhelming. We no longer have any **certainty** about the right way to live, who to trust or what is true. Jobs tend not to be permanent, relationships are temporary: everything is **fluid**. This leads to a lot of anxiety, especially as all our choices come with great **risk**.

Fluidity means that the distinction between children and Youth is breaking down, as is the difference between Youth and adulthood. Instead, adults increasingly participate in Youth Culture as do children. This was recognised by **Postman (*The Disappearance of Childhood*, 1994**, p83)**.

'Death of Meta-Narratives': Part of this uncertainty is that the old explanations for things no longer satisfy people. These **'meta-narratives'** (or 'Big Stories') include religious teachings, political theories and **structuralist sociological Perspectives** like Marxism and Functionalism and even science itself. **Jean-Francois Lyotard (1979)** argues that the world has become too chaotic and changeable to be explicable by just one grand theory.

This means that Marxist ideas about **resisting Capitalism (Hebdige, 1979**, p53) or Functionalist ideas about **Meritocracy (Davis & Moore, 1945**, p60) are no longer credible explanations for Youth Culture.

Many sociologists accept there have been huge changes in society, but deny they amount to shift to Postmodernity. **Anthony Giddens (*Runaway World*, 1999**, p24)** argues we are living **in Late Modernity**, the latest stage of modernity, characterised by extreme choice and risk, but still with much in common with previous generations.

> **Research:** Go back over your notes on **Section A** and review **Global Culture, multiculturalism, Intersectional Identity** and the ideas of **Baudrillard, Davis & Moore, Faludi, Giddens, Hebdige** and **Postman** mentioned above, adding this Postmodern Perspective to them.

YOUTH CULTURE: A TOOLKIT

Youth Culture means the distinctive lifestyle of young people (teenagers). Youth Culture includes things like teenage food and drink, youth fashions and haircuts, teenage attitudes to politics or morality, pop music, video games, 'Young Adult' literature, movies & TV shows aimed at this audience, social media platforms preferred by young people and the sport they enjoy, as well as teenage etiquette, the drugs and sexual behaviour they think are acceptable.

AO2 ILLUSTRATION: YOUTH ONLINE

Whereas adults still watch the BBC or streaming services like Netflix, **YouTube** is the favourite for teenagers, with **Snapchat** and **Instagram** being more popular with teens than Facebook (preferred by their parents). New platforms like **TikTok** and **Twitch** are gaining popularity with young people. Young people are drawn to **vloggers** who post on these sites (also known as '**micro-influences'**) and there has been a rise in **social activism** online among young people, which has been nicknamed '**the Greta Effect'** after teenage environmental activist Greta Thunberg.

12-15 year olds
- 83% have their own smartphone
- 59% have their own tablet
- 81% use a smartphone to go online, **and** 69% use a tablet to go online
- 74% who own a mobile phone are allowed to take it to bed with them, while 61% of tablet owners are allowed to do this
- 36% use a smart speaker in the home
- 88% watch TV on a TV set, while 46% use a tablet, and 41% use a mobile phone to watch TV
- 98% watch TV programmes or films (on any device), for 11hrs 48mins a week
- 75% watch live broadcast TV, and 88% watch video-on-demand content⁺
- 81% play games, for 11hrs 36mins a week
- 72% play games online
- 89% watch YouTube, for 11hrs a week
- 41% watch YouTubers or vloggers
- 71% of online users have a social media profile

Source: Ofcom (2019)

Consensus vs Conflict

Functionalists see Youth as a necessary stage between childhood and adulthood. It is necessary because young people must be **integrated into society**. Children are socialised by their **family** and adults by the families they start (p38) and their **workplace** (p45) but young people are mostly socialised by their **peers** (p40).

Talcott Parsons (p35) argues that, in a complex Capitalist society, young people need to be 'eased into' their adult roles. They take part-time jobs in preparation for careers, they date boyfriends or girlfriends in preparation for marriage, they loosen their ties to their parents in preparation for becoming fully independent: Youth is a period of preparation.

This is a **Consensus view** because it focuses on young people joining the wider community, learning its **norms and values** and figuring out how to fit in. It downplays the **deviant** behaviour of young people ("youthful high spirits!") and ignores the extent to which young people are **exploited** by employers and advertisers, **sexually predated upon** and the amount of depression and self-harm young people experience.

Marxists see Youth as an artificial category created by Capitalism. For example, the word "teenager" dates from the 1940s and was coined by American advertisers who had noticed the spending power of this age group and wanted to sell them comics, music, movies, cosmetics and (in America) cars.

Karl Marx argues that Capitalism creates **alienation** from your work and yourself (p46) and young people are experiencing this alienation for the first time and, in their different ways, try to **resist** it.

This is a **Conflict view** because it sees young people as the victims of a sort of Capitalist conspiracy to turn them into consumers – and then into obedient workers who need a wage to fund their consumption habits. Youth deviance and mental ill-health is a side-effect of this alienation. However, this view downplays the positive experiences that many young people have in part-time work and dating: the skills and responsibilities they learn at work, the emotional growth from teenage romance.

Feminists argue that young women are not just under pressure to accept their role as workers in the Capitalist economy, but a subordinate role too, oppressed by men. They learn to accept being sexually objectified (viewed as bodies for the sexual please of men), sexually harassed in the street and the workplace and subjected to sexual bullying by boyfriends. Much of this is catalogued in **Laura Bates' Everyday Sexism Project** (**2012**, https://everydaysexism.com/).

The *Sturm und Drang* ('Storm & Stress' p97) of Youth can be viewed from either angle. Consensus sees it as part of a difficult transition to adulthood and the emotional wrenching of breaking ties with parents and childhood security; Conflict sees it as a response to exploitation and the alienation of life in a Capitalist society that is only soothed by the brainwashing of **ruling class ideology**.

AO2 ILLUSTRATION: EVERYDAY SEXISM

Laura Bates worked as a nanny in her 20s but found the girls she looked after were strangely preoccupied with their body image and this was linked to the treatment they received in public and at school. She set up the **Everyday Sexism Project** in April 2012. She hoped to gather a hundred stories of sexual harassment in daily life, but her website quickly collected thousands and exceeded 100,000 testimonials in its first 3 years. Many of the stories were from young girls, including a 9-year-old who was sent a "dick pic" on her phone and many stories of being groped on public transport or verbally abused by passing strangers. Bates argues this behaviour is **normalised**: we accept it as normal, even though we shouldn't.

Bates herself received many death threats and rape threats. She writes in 2017: *"To be a feminist, I have learned, is to be accused of oversensitivity, hysteria and crying wolf. But in the face of the abuse the project uncovered, the sheer strength, ingenuity and humour of women shone like a beacon."*

2012 is usually taken to be the beginning of the **4th Wave of Feminism**, which is focused on online activism and **Intersectionality** (p63). Laura Bates' project is at the forefront of this. However, critics like **Germaine Greer (2014)** point out that much of the material on the Everyday Sexism website isn't sexist behaviour that has become normalised, but rather it is widespread criminal behaviour that isn't reported or punished.

AO2 ILLUSTRATION: THE ICE BUCKET CHALLENGE

This Challenge went viral on social media in the summer of 2014, started by US baseball player Peter Frates who was diagnosed with motor neurone disease (called ALS in America). The challenger tags a friend online, who must post up a video of themselves being doused with a bucket of icy water within 24 hours and challenge someone else. Typically, they must donate £100 to the medical charity, or just £10 if they perform the Challenge – although in some versions they pay nothing if they do the challenge and only pay if they decline it.

The Challenge raised £200 million worldwide and there were 2.4 million tagged videos on Facebook. Although celebrities and world leaders got involved, the Challenge was hugely popular among young people and spread by Youth Culture.

From a Consensus view, this shows shared moral values (giving to charity, supporting the sick) and introduces young people to charity activities. From a Conflict viewpoint, the Challenge is more of a stunt with the focus on narcissism (showing off) – the fact that many performers did the stunt *instead of* donating to charity makes it **'slacktivism'** (supporting a good cause with minimal commitment). It was also criticised for wasting water – 5 million gallons were used in 2014 at the same time as California was suffering a drought.

Online Youth Culture like this is a good example of a Postmodern Perspective: an obsession with media images is Hyper Reality becoming more important than real life.

RESEARCH PROFILE: EISENSTADT (1956)

Shmuel Eistenstadt (1923-2010) was a colleague of Talcott Parsons and his book *From Generation To Generation* (1956) develops Parsons' ideas further.

Eisenstadt accepts the Functionalist idea of **Sturm und Drang** ('storm & stress' in adolescence, p97) and links this to **anomie** (p10) brought on by isolation. Youth Culture and especially a peer group gives adolescents a vital sense of **belonging** (**social integration**).

Youth culture also allows adolescents to 'let off steam' in a safe way and **transgressive behaviour** (breaking the rules) by them is tolerated by society as part of 'youthful high spirits.' These transgressions are also important ways for young people to test the boundaries and experiment with norms and values. Ultimately, youthful transgressive behaviour contributes to social order by helping adolescents settle down as responsible adults.

A standard criticism of Parsons and Eisenstadt is that they were **middle class white males** writing in the 1950s. Their views only ever described a privileged section of society and, given the social changes since then (such as increasing **multiculturalism** and **Global Culture**), they might not apply to any section of society today.

However, Eisenstadt is not American but Israeli and Israel is a country with conscription of young people into the military at age 18. This might weaken Eisenstadt's arguments – or the similarity in his findings to the American Parsons might strengthen his claim to have identified universal functions of Youth Culture.

Research: other online youth trends and crazes (like Planking, Momo, Kylie Lips, Bottle Flipping, Blue Whale); youth protest movements or activism; trends/statistics for youth working & wages; visit the Everyday Sexism Project at https://everydaysexism.com/ and read the testimonies

Social Order & Control

Social Control (p38) is the way that society gets people to conform to mainstream norms and values. This is done through the **Agencies of Social Control** covered in **Section A**. These agencies can be **formal** (like the police) or **informal** (like peer groups).

Young people are in many ways quite easy to control. They tend to live with their parents who monitor their behaviour. They are compelled to attend school. They do not have much money, depend on public transport and laws prevent them from doing many activities (like buying alcohol). Shops often only allow young people to enter in small groups and the police tell groups of youngsters to 'move along.' In addition, adults monitor young people informally and tend to report groups of youths 'loitering.'

Notice we have a special word for young people socialising in public places – 'loitering' implies they are up to no good. You never hear of elderly people being spotted 'loitering' in a park.

Young people find ways to avoid this social control. They often don't tell their parents where they are going and parents have trouble monitoring what their children are doing online. School is compulsory up to 18, but young people truant. Bicycles help young people get about and in Italy young people can travel on mopeds from age 14 – a striking part of Italian Youth Culture, especially as the requirement to get a licence was only introduced in 2004. Young people respond to monitoring with fashions that hide their identity, particularly hoodies.

A big **class difference** comes into effect, because middle class youths can meet and socialise at home: they have their own bedrooms and their parents have large houses where they can enjoy some privacy. They are more likely to have money to get into venues or travel and more likely to drive cars.

Working class youths often don't have homes that are large or private enough for this, or the money to go to other venues or drive cars. They are forced to socialise in public places, which means they draw attention and social control.

Feminists point out that young women are subjected to much more social control than males. This is largely informal, from family and peer groups: being labelled as a 'slag' is much more shaming for a girl than a boy. Parents monitor who their daughters befriend and date more closely than their sons. At the same time, sexually abusive behaviour from boys and young men is not challenged or punished (*c.f.* the **Everyone's Invited** website discussed in **Section** A, p40).

AO2 ILLUSTRATION: NATIONAL SERVICE VS NCS

After World War II, young men aged 18-21 were required to serve in the military for 18 months. This was called 'National Service' and it lasted until 1960. These conscripts took part in military action in Malaya, Kenya and the Korean War. National Service acted as a **'rite of passage'** marking the end of Youth. For years afterwards, it was said of delinquent youths that *"some National Service would do 'em good!"* Recently **Prince Harry (2015)** has called for the reintroduction of National Service, saying: *"the army has done amazing things for me."* Norway, Sweden and Israel are countries that still have compulsory military service for young men and women.

In 2011, the **National Citizenship Service (NCS)** was launched as a non-military (and non-compulsory) alternative to National Service. Groups of 16-17 year olds take a residential course, do physical and team building activities, learn life skills then plan and deliver a project to benefit the community. In 2018, more than 400,000 young people had taken part.

*I hope you can see the **Functionalist** thinking behind NCS and the idea that National Service would be 'good for young people.'*

Of course, **Marxists** are opposed to the idea of young people being conscripted into the Armed Forces and NCS is criticised for being too expensive for working class children and being a propaganda course for **ruling class ideology (Tania de St Croix, 2017)**.

RESEARCH PROFILE: CHAMBLISS (1973)

In 1973, **William Chambliss** published *The Saints & the Roughnecks*, an article describing two years spent observing Hannibal High School students (age 16-19) in America. He followed two gangs: six working class Roughnecks and eight middle class Saints. (The names of the gangs and the school are fictional to protect the anonymity of the boys and their families).

Chambliss observed that the Saints' behaviour was in many ways *worse* than the Roughnecks, engaging in truancy, under-age drinking, dangerous driving and vandalism. Yet they were seen as model students, whereas the Roughnecks were constantly in trouble with teachers and the police.

The Saints were successful in school, viewed as 'good students' by the teachers and found it easy to truant by pretending to have extracurricular activities. Since they had cars, they could travel to other suburbs or into the city to misbehave, where no one would recognise them. When they got into trouble with the police, they could pay fines and their parents would vouch for them.

The Roughnecks were viewed as delinquents. Their truancy was lower than the Saints, but it was public knowledge. Without cars, they had to gather in their own neighbourhood, where their fighting and drunkenness was observed. There were in trouble with the police and, while Chambliss observed them, each Roughneck was arrested at least once.

Chambliss uses **Labelling Theory** to explain his findings: the Saints had positive labels so their behaviour was interpreted as harmless; the Roughnecks were interpreted as delinquent because of their negative labels. The Saints went on to college and good jobs. The Roughnecks had different outcomes: attempted suicide, prison, gambling, unemployment.

Chambliss connects this to a **Marxist** understanding of class and privilege. Social control is imposed on the working classes, but not the middle classes, and this control *creates* deviancy rather than reducing it.

Chambliss' study is from the 1970s and the USA, so the results might not apply to 21st century schoolboys or the UK, where teenagers don't drive until they are 18 but they can legally buy alcohol before they are 21. The arrival of the Internet has changed the way young people socialise. The boys were white, so the study doesn't tell us about other ethnic groups or girls. The small sample size, although typical of **Interactionist** research, is hard to generalise from: these could have been unusual teenagers at an unusual school.

*Chambliss' study makes a great comparison for **Willis'** Learning To Labour (1973, p41) where 'the Lads' behave similarly to Chambliss' Roughnecks (although they are a year or two younger). It is also interesting to compare with the Spur Posse observed by **Faludi** in **Stiffed** (1991, p75).*

Research: respectable public figures with deviancy in their youth (e.g. Brett Kavanaugh in USA; David Cameron in UK); celebrities shamed by social media posts made in their teens; transgressive behaviour at elite private schools (e.g. www.everyonesinvited.uk/)

EXAM PRACTICE: YOUTH CULTURE

The OCR exam has three questions in **Paper 1 Section B**. Questions 4-6 are on Families & Relationships and questions 10-12 are on the Media, but this Study Guide is focused on Option 2, which contains questions 7-9:

4. Outline two explanations for the formation of youth culture. **[12 marks: 8 AO1 + 4 AO2]**

This is very similar to Q2 in Section A, but with no source A and B, so it has to come entirely from your own learning. Notice that the importance of AO1 and AO2 is switched: you get more marks for knowledge of Sociology here and far fewer for real life illustrations.

*Make **two sociological points** about youth culture – perhaps from a Consensus and a Conflict viewpoint. Each point should have its own paragraph and be supported by evidence from a named sociologist or piece of research. You have 10 minutes to write this.*

5. Explain and briefly evaluate the view that youth culture is a form of social control. **[16 marks: 8 AO1 + 4 AO2 + 4 AO3]**

*This is similar to Q3 in Section A, but again with fewer marks given to AO2 illustration. The advice on writing evaluation from **1A Socialisation, Culture & Identity** applies here.*

*Write three paragraphs: **two argue in favour** of the question and the **third paragraph argues against** (e.g. that youth is a period of rebellion or resistance rather than social control). For example, you could write about the **Functionalist** idea of youth culture as preparation, **Eisenstadt's theory of testing boundaries and venting frustration** (p108) but finish off with the Marxist idea of youth as symbolic resistance to Capitalism. You have 15 minutes for this.*

6. Assess feminist views about the role of youth culture. **[24 marks: 8 AO1 + 8 AO2 + 8 AO3]**

*This is a brand new style of question, with equal weight given to knowledge of Sociology, illustration and evaluation. The evaluation has to be developed evaluation; see **Chapter 9** for advice on this.*

*Write three paragraphs. Each paragraph should introduce a sociological idea with some illustration from the real world. Each paragraph should finish off with a developed evaluation (see Chapter 9 for this). For example, you could write about the idea of youth culture socialising girls into heteronormative roles, then the idea of youth culture helping young women to resist patriarchy, then finish off with **Laura Bates' Everyday Sexism Project** (p107) which exposes how widespread sexual harassment is.*

CHAPTER SIX – YOUTH SUBCULTURES

Subcultures were introduced in **Section A** (p24) as a 'group within a group' that shares some of the **norms and values** of mainstream society but has norms and values of its own that might be seen as **deviant** (or at least unusual) by mainstream society.

In a way, Youth Culture is one gigantic subculture within society. When teenage Youth Culture was observed in the USA and UK in the 1950s, many commentators were disturbed by the appearance of this 'group within a group.' The phrase **'the Generation Gap'** was coined to refer to the difference between mainstream norms and values and the 'storm & stress' of teenage life, which seemed to be wild, irresponsible and sexually unrestrained.

Youth Subcultures quickly emerged within Youth Culture itself: the **Teddy Boys** of the 1950s (p134), the **Mods** (p120), **Rockers** and **Hippies** of the '70s and the **Skinheads** (p119) and **Punks** (p140) of the '70s. Later, **Goths** (p127), **Emos**, **Ravers** and other groups appeared, mostly linked to popular music. More recently, **Geek** (p117) subcultures linked to gaming, comics and computing have appeared.

Positive Views of Youth Subcultures

Youth Subcultures create an intense sense of belonging within a peer group. Because of the shared interest and often recognisable dress code, the subculture finds it easy to identify one another and integrate. Subcultures often draw in some of the most isolated or alienated young people who struggle to find a place within wider Youth Culture.

Subcultures can help young people with mental health problems, bullying, poverty or family abuse by offering supportive peers and a 'home away from home.' Some subcultures can also be involved in social activism, joining in protests and encouraging young people to question things mainstream society takes for granted.

Negative Views of Youth Subcultures

There's always a concern that Youth Culture separates young people from mainstream norms and values, but youth subcultures intensify this: they can be outright deviant. This can lead to young people being labelled as 'weirdos' and also bring them into contact with criminals (e.g. drug dealers) and trouble with the police.

Some youth subcultures reject Consumer Culture (e.g. **Punks**, p140) but others are strongly linked to it, meaning that youth subcultures can be a way for Capitalism to exploit young people by selling them products (music, fashion, the latest video games).

RESEARCH PROFILE: THE CENTRE FOR CONTEMPORARY CULTURAL STUDIES (CCCS, 1970s)

The **CCCS** was a research centre at the University of Birmingham, focused on **Neo-Marxist** Sociology – taking Marxist ideas about class conflict but using **Gramsci**'s idea about **Hegemony** rather than the traditional ruling class. It also used many techniques developed by **Interactionism** (p116) such as participant observation of small groups and **moral panics** (p148) in the Media.

It was founded in 1964 by **Stuart Hall** and continued working until 2002, but it is best known for its work on Youth Subcultures in the 1970s.

The CCCS publications included **Paul *Willis' Learning To Labour* (1977**, p41**)** which studied 'the Lads' and **Dick Hebdige**'s *Subculture: The Meaning of Style* (1979, p140**)** which analysed Punks.

A major CCCS publication was the collection *Resistance Through Rituals* **(ed. Hall & Jefferson, 1976)**. This book proposed the idea that Youth Subcultures formed from working class youngsters resisting Capitalism and that much of the music, fashion and behaviour of youth subcultures needs to be interpreted as a rejection of Capitalist values and a commitment to **Working Class Identity**.

Contributors included **John Clarke** and **Phil Cohen** on Skinheads (p119), **Dick Hebdige** on Mods and **Tony Jefferson** (p135) on 1950s Teddy Boys.

A lot of this research involves **semiology**, which is a technique for interpreting **codes** (symbolic behaviour). For example, semiology is used to interpret Punk dress, language and music as resistance to Capitalism – but is it just delighting in shocking people? The problem with semiology is that the researcher's theoretical Perspective (i.e. Marxism) determines how the researcher 'reads' the codes and it's not obvious which reading is correct.

The CCCS researched at a time when the UK was rocked by conflict, with military attacks in Northern Ireland, mass unemployment, general strikes and later (in the 1980s) battles between police and strikers. These social circumstances might explain the youth subcultures that appeared, but they also might make the CCCS's ideas irrelevant now. However, supporters would argue these conflicts still exist in society, but in new forms (e.g. employment is now high, but many people work in the 'gig economy' for low wages and no security).

Research: find out about a youth subculture: Teddy Boys, Hippies, Mods, Rockers/Bikers, Skinheads, Punks, Goths, Emos, Ravers, Crusties – or a contemporary UK musical subculture like Drill, Grime or Makina; revisit your notes from **Section A** to place **Willis (1977)** in context

PERSPECTIVES ON YOUTH SUBCULTURES

Views on the importance and value of Youth Subcultures go to the heart of what makes the Perspectives different. They reveal a lot about views on **Consensus**, **Conflict** and **Social Order**.

CONSENSUS PERSPECTIVE: FUNCTIONALISM

Functionalism sees Youth Subcultures as part of the **transition** from family to workplace, which is a change from a loving and personal world where you are valued for who you are to a cold and impersonal one where you are valued for what you can do. Youth Culture in general helps with this transition, providing a sense of belonging to oppose **anomie**, but for some young people the transition is particularly difficult. These tend to be boys and working class, because boys are more likely to move into full-time work (as opposed to motherhood) and working-class people are more likely to work in dangerous impersonal conditions, like factories.

You can see the rather dated Functionalist ideas here: in the 21st century, working-class people don't all work in factories and women don't automatically become housewives and mothers.

These pressures lead boys – especially working-class boys – to create subcultures to ease the transition further. In a nutshell, because a bigger change is required of them, they have to make a bigger break with their childhood. Subcultures are a type of **adaptation** to difficult circumstances, like the cocoon a caterpillar enters to emerge as a butterfly.

Feminists criticise this view for the *"invisibility of women"* in it. **Marxists** argue that working class subcultures are about **resisting Capitalism**, not adapting to it.

This Functionalist view explains why most young people *don't* join subcultures and why older people *grow out of* their subcultures – but it fails to explain why particular subcultures take the forms they do (why do Skinheads shave their heads and wear workmen's boots? why do Punks wear torn clothes and spike their hair?).

Functionalism has an ambivalent (muddled, divided) attitude to subcultures. On the one hand, they are necessary phases in growing up for some people. On the other hand, they show a lot of **dysfunctional behaviour** and suggest a **failure of socialisation**, especially among the working class. Functionalism doesn't have a definite answer on whether Youth Subcultures are a **threat to social order** or a harmless (and ultimately beneficial) phase.

CONFLICT PERSPECTIVE: MARXISM

Marxism sees Youth Culture as a mixture of **exploitation** by and **resistance** to Capitalism. Youth Subcultures are seen as pure **resistance**. This is especially true of the subcultures studied by the **CCCS** in the 1960s and '70s, which were termed **Spectacular Youth Subcultures** (p139) because of their dramatic styles.

Middle-class youngsters find it easy to 'play by the rules' in society because of their class position: they have **privileges** and don't encounter **oppression** or obstacles. Working-class youngsters don't enjoy these privileges. Moreover, in the 1960s and '70s the industrial basis of working-class life was changing: factories were closing and unemployment rising. Education claimed to be a **Meritocracy** for working-class children but didn't offer **social mobility** for most of them. These young people perceive the Capitalist system to be a cheat and a lie and reject it; instead, they emphasise their **Working Class Identity**.

This analysis involves **semiology**: interpreting the codes of fashion and behaviour in symbolic ways. For example, wearing heavy denims and workingmen's boots is a code for **Working Class Identity**; wearing torn or homemade clothes is a code for rejecting **Consumer Culture**.

Feminists also complain about the *"invisibility of women"* in this Perspective. **Functionalists** point out that the conclusions of semiology reflect the researcher's starting point: if you start out *assuming* that subcultures are resisting Capitalism, you 'read' the codes to prove this. But this isn't really 'proof' and the codes could be 'read' in other ways.

Marxism also fails to explain why most young people *don't* join subcultures and why so many grow out of them in a few years. However, it does explain (through semiology) why the subcultures take the particular form they do.

CONFLICT PERSPECTIVE: FEMINISM

Feminists complain about the *"invisibility of women"* in studies of Youth Subculture. On the face of it, there *seem* to be more boys than girls in Spectacular Youth Subcultures, but this is for two reasons: (1) the researchers of the CCCS are **mostly male** and drawn to the more violent masculine behaviour in subcultures (**androcentric** or 'male-centred' **bias**), and (2) girls are **more socially controlled** by parents and teachers and attract **more negative labelling** for their deviant behaviour.

For example, there is a **double-standard** that makes it more acceptable for males to be outrageous or transgressive but females are condemned for doing this – even by the deviant males.

Feminists argue there is a **'bedroom culture'** for girls that exists in the privacy of the home. Girls can indulge in subcultural behaviour here (such as indulging in sexual fantasies about teen idols) while maintaining their reputation in public. This analysis also involves **semiology**, which has similar problems to Marxist analysis. It is much harder to gather **empirical** (fact-based) **evidence** about bedroom culture, because it isn't going on in public.

If social control of females weakens, you would expect female subcultures to move out of the bedroom and into the public sphere. This might explain the appearance of **'Ladettes'** in the 1990s (p74).

SOCIAL ACTION PERSPECTIVE: INTERACTIONISM

Interactionists reject the sort of structuralist explanations presented so far, like the idea that entire classes of people are behaving a certain way because of social forces. From an Interactionist viewpoint, Youth Subcultures *don't really exist*. Instead, there is a 'hard core' of innovative young people creating their own style (e.g. the 'true punks') and then a huge number of copycats who temporarily imitate aspects of that subculture, usually because the Media made it look interesting or glamorous.

This approach uses the idea of **societal reaction**. The Media picks on a few unconnected cases of young people producing unusual music or wearing exotic fashions. These cases really have nothing to do with each other, but the Media pulls them together in an **ideological framework** (an 'explanation that makes sense'), giving the phenomenon a title like 'punk.' All the people dressing like that or enjoying music like that are now labelled 'punks' even though they previously never saw themselves as a subculture.

A **Self-Fulfilling Prophecy (SFP)** takes place, as young people act out the labels and internalise them as a sense of **Identity**. Often, the Media fuels public outrage, which strengthens the sense of Identity. Eventually, the Media loses interest and, without it, the 'subculture' dissolves.

Interactionism is a good explanation of the Media's role in the formation of Youth Subcultures – see **Chapter 8** for a more detailed look at this. However, it is accused of being a *description* of subcultures forming rather than an *explanation*. For example, why does the Media single out certain individuals or groups in the first place? where does the ideological framework tying these behaviours together come from? why does the Media stir up outrage rather than, say, curiosity or admiration?

Marxists like **Stuart Hall** (**1978**, p131) claim to have the answer to this: the Media has a structural relationship to Capitalist institutions, so it regularly scapegoats young people to blame them for crises in Capitalism. The Interactionist account is incomplete without Marxism.

POSTMODERN PERSPECTIVE: POSTMODERNISM

Postmodernists agree with Interactionists that structuralist explanations of Youth Subcultures are implausible: they are **'Meta-Narratives'** that no longer make sense in a **fragmented** world. They also agree that the Media is involved, although they do not regard the Media as a **hegemonic** (leading, directing) force that provides a single ideological framework for things. In the 21st century, the Media is vast but fragmented, with people accessing different things online rather than reading the same things in newspapers.

Instead, Postmodernists argue we live in a **media-saturated society** and a **Hyper-Reality** where media images are more important than real events. We construct our identities from these media images, visiting what **Ted Polhemus (1997)** calls **'the Supermarket of Style**.'

This means that Youth Subcultures are becoming a thing of the past. Young people can pick and choose different style elements for their identity, like a collage: a bit of punk, a bit of geek, some hippie-chic. Polhemus argues that young people aren't willing to commit to one particular style and restrict their choices. Moreover, style is based on what people discover in the Media, rather than on their experiences in the real world away from Hyper Reality.

Michel Maffesoli (1996, p124**)** argues that subcultures have been replaced by more fluid **Neo-Tribes**.

As usual, Postmodernism is fascinating but imprecise. The Spectacular Youth Subcultures *do* seem to have faded but **Goths** (p127) are still with us and the **Geek Subculture** (p117) is flourishing. A generic sort of Youth Culture seems to have arisen, based around the Internet, night clubs, video games, etc. However, families and education still socialise people and Capitalism still exists: we don't live our entire lives online and we're not free to create any Identity we like, particularly if we are poor and working class.

AO2 ILLUSTRATION: GEEKS

The Geek Subculture is based around enthusiasm for obscure media (Japanese animation, video games, comic books, etc.) and includes activities such as role-playing games (e.g. *Dungeons and Dragons*), science fiction (e.g. *Star Trek*) and new technology.

Geek interests used to be marginalised in the 1970s and '80s but have become more mainstream. Comic book movie adaptations (e.g. *Marvel*) are now massive cinema hits. Science-fiction and fantasy-themed video games (e.g. *World of Warcraft*) have become multi-billion dollar industries and former-Geeks like **Steve Jobs** and **Bill Gates** have become influential billionaires. The first **San Diego Comic-Con** in 1970 drew 100 people; today the convention attracts 130,000 and major companies launch products there (like trailers for forthcoming movies). The TV sitcom *The Big Bang Theory* (2007-19) popularised Geek Subculture but also the stereotype of Geeks having poor social skills.

Mark Roeder (2014) argues that Geeks are in fact the next stage in human evolution: *"the high-tech environment … favours people with geek-like traits, many of whom are on the autism spectrum, ADHD, or dyslexia. Previously, such people may have been at a disadvantage, but now their unique cognitive traits enable some of them to resonate with the new technological zeitgeist and become very successful."*

Unlike the **Spectacular Youth Subcultures** that fascinate Marxists (p139), the Geek Subculture is more middle-class and associated with academically-successful but socially-excluded young people. Its links to the Internet, imaginary worlds and role-playing link it to **Postmodernism**, as a subculture formed by **media-saturation** and **Hyper-Reality**.

Feminists complain that the Geek Subculture is often sexist and the term **'Geek Girl'** has become an insult among male Geeks, suggesting a woman who fakes an interest in Geek topics to gain attention.

YOUTH SUBCULTURES: A TOOLKIT

Youth Subcultures can be understood in relation to some of the aspects of **Identity** you learned about in **Section A**.

YOUTH SUBCULTURES RELATED TO SOCIAL CLASS

This is the most common Identity related to subcultures. **Functionalists** and **Marxists** both see Class Identity as important for forming youth subcultures. For Functionalists, this is to help working class boys (in particular) adapt to their role in a Capitalist **Meritocracy**.

For Marxists, this is an insight into the **exploitative** nature of Capitalism, **resistance** to its values and a defiant statement of **Working Class Identity** (p76). Most Marxist research into this assumes that there is something *misguided* about Youth Subcultures: these young people are concerned about very real problems faced by working class communities that aren't being addressed by politicians or the mainstream media, but they express these concerns in unhelpful ways (e.g. through violence, fashion or music).

Functionalists are more inclined to explain the violence and deviancy through poor **Primary Socialisation** in the family (p35) and poor **Secondary Socialisation** (p37) due to failing schools, the decline of religion and the rise of unemployment. For Functionalists, these subcultures aren't trying to make a muddled political statement, they're just behaving badly due to *Sturm und Drang* (p97).

Both Perspectives can be criticised for failing to address middle class Youth Subcultures, such as Hippies or Sloanes.

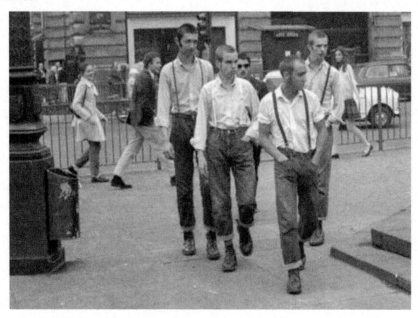

AO2 ILLUSTRATION: SKINHEADS

This Youth Subculture is famous for shaved heads, but also work boots (originally army surplus, later Doc Martens), jeans, braces and buttoned-down shirts. The 'uniform' represents working class pride.

There were two 'waves' of Skinhead subcultures. The first, in the 1960s, grew out of the Mod Subculture. These Skinheads (or 'Skins') listened to soul, ska and rocksteady (reggae) music – strongly influenced by the music of the Caribbean immigrants of the **Windrush Generation**. This mixing of White working class and Black Caribbean culture is a form of **Hybridity**.

A second wave of Skinhead Subcultures happened in the late 1970s, in response to Punk. These Skinheads listened to 2-Tone music (combining Ska and Punk) and were drawn into Far Right and White Supremacist politics – which is ironic, since Caribbean immigration influenced the first wave of Skinheads. However, there were anti-racist Skinheads who opposed these developments.

Research: listen to ska and rocksteady music like that of Desmond Dekker; find out about Hippies and/or Sloanes

RESEARCH PROFILE: CLARKE, COHEN (1976)

John Clarke and **Phil Cohen** were both sociologists from the CCCS and contributed to *Resistance Through Rituals* (1976). Both use **semiology** to explore how Skinhead Subcultures of the 1960s and early '70s express their norms and values through **codes**.

Clarke argues that Skinheads feel their working-class community is under attack from Capitalism (through unemployment, changing work patterns, immigration, etc.) and respond by adopting an exaggeratedly working-class and masculine appearance, based on the industrial and factory dress styles of their parents and grandparents.

Cohen argues that Skinheads is essentially territorial and based on the perception that working class areas are being lost because of Asian immigration. They oppose this symbolically through football hooliganism, which Cohen argues is meant to express ownership of the territory around the football ground. Cohen suggests that Skinhead violence is **symbolic resistance to social change** and an attempt to **'magically'** recreate a working-class community. These are 'magical' because they offer young people a sense of strength and power but no practical solutions.

There's nothing very pretty about football hooliganism or racist violence. The tendency of Clarke and Cohen to reinterpret this as something noble or tragic (working class youths yearning for a lost community) should alert you to a problem with Neo-Marxist semiology: there's a risk of downplaying racism and hooliganism and portraying bad people as heroes.

YOUTH SUBCULTURES RELATED TO GENDER

Secondary Socialisation is the later influence of other people on your social experience. Children are influenced by their teachers, but also by youth leaders, religious leaders and later by employers. Peer groups (friends) and the media (TV, the Internet, pop music, video games) also affect our norms and values. The socialisation that continues into adulthood (for example, in the workplace) is sometimes termed **Tertiary Socialisation** (tertiary means "third").

As noticed by Feminists like **Anne Oakley** (p39), young women are socialised differently from young men and are often encouraged to be passive, attractive and compliant. This makes it more difficult for them to participate in antisocial youth subcultures, especially if the subcultures are violent. One subculture that proved popular with young women in the 1960s and '70s was Mods.

AO2 ILLUSTRATION: MODS

This Youth Subculture is famous for close-cropped hair, smart shirts, thin ties and tailor-made suits. The 'unform' emphasises style and a good taste. Mods were associated with mopeds, especially stylish Italian scooters like Vespa.

Mods had an **androgynous** look (mixing masculine and feminine features). Some male Mods wore lipstick and eyeshadow and some female Mods who wore men's trousers, flat shoes, very short hair and little makeup

Fashion designer **Mary Quant** invented the miniskirt and made Mod fashion mainstream. Women were drawn to the Mod Subculture because of the focus on style which made it easy to combine membership of the subculture with ordinary participation in work and school but also because it avoided the drunkenness and violence of other Youth Subcultures.

They were also associated with using amphetamines (not illegal in the UK in the 1960s); the drug is a stimulant which helped Mods stay up late socialising in coffee shops (British pubs all closed at 11pm but coffee shops often had live music). Early Mods listened to Modern Jazz and Blues, but later bands like The Who and Small Faces. The was a 'Mod Revival' in the 1970s led by The Jam.

Research: listen to music popular with Mods: the Modern Jazz Quartet, The Kinks, The Who, Small Faces as well as the 1970s Mod revival music like The Jam

RESEARCH PROFILE: McROBBIE & GARBER (1976)

Angela McRobbie & Jenny Garber were published as part of *Resistance Through Rituals* (1976) but they criticised the **CCCS** for ignoring the role of women in favour of the male-dominated Spectacular Youth Subcultures. Male CCCS researchers tended to treat the girls as passive hangers-on.

McRobbie & Garber focus on one subculture where girls were quite prominent: the **Mod** Subculture. Mods placed importance on smart, fashionable clothing and the close-cropped hair created an androgynous (mixing masculine and feminine) look, making males and females appear similar. However, in the 1970s, girls experienced a **sexual double-standard** that meant even Mod males judged them harshly if the girls engaged in deviant behaviour.

Instead, the researchers focus on another female subculture called **Teenyboppers**. These teenage girls enjoyed pop music, focusing on 'teenage heart-throb' celebrities and girls' magazines (especially *Jackie*). The term 'bedroom culture' describes this private world where girls would meet at home, enjoy sleepovers ('pyjama parties') share magazines, experiment with fashion and makeup and gossip about boys. McRobbie & Garber argue that this is just as much **symbolic resistance to hegemonic Gender Identity** as the public behaviour of the boys; in the bedroom, the girls share taboo subjects (like sexual desire) and experiment with changing their appearance and Identity.

Critics argue that all girls are doing in the bedrooms is passively consuming media products like posters and magazines. McRobbie argues that this isn't so and girls are **active consumers**, resisting stereotypes and constructing their own **Gender** (p74), **Class** (p76), **Ethnic** (p69) and **Sexual Identities** (p79).

YOUTH SUBCULTURES RELATED TO ETHNICITY

British Youth Culture has been influenced by immigrants, starting with the Windrush Generation. Both Mod and Skinhead culture developed out of Caribbean and Black American music. Ethnic minorities themselves are encouraged to **assimilate** and resemble the dominant White culture or engage in **cultural defence** and exaggerate features of the own culture.

Dick Hebdige (*Subculture: The Meaning of Style*, 1979) views Black Reggae and Rastafarian Subcultures as equally **resistance** to White culture and racism (p140).

Similarly, **Sanjiev Johal** (*Brimful of Brasia*, 1998) sees British Asians ('**Brasians**') as taking on a **'hyper-ethnic' style** to exaggerate their differences from the White community (by watching Bollywood cinema, listening to Bhangra music, etc.).

AO2 ILLUSTRATION: HIP-HOP

Hip-Hop grew out of Black American Culture in New York in the 1970s. The founders were **DJ Kool Herc** (who pioneered DJing with mixing decks and rapping), **Afrika Bambaataa** (who added break dancing and visual art with a spiritual philosophy) and **Grandmaster Flash** (who introduced scratching and other techniques for speeding and reversing the beats). This brought together the 4 Pillars of Hip-Hop Culture: (1) **DJing**, (2) **breaking dancing**, (3) **rapping**, and (4) **graffiti**.

The 'Golden Age of Hip-Hop' was the 1980s and '90s, when Rap music moved into the mainstream, distinguished by its use of sampling sound clips of movies and other songs. Copyright laws were brought in to restrict this style.

Hip-Hop fashion also became mainstream: baggy shirts, trainers and urban hairstyles. Street slang, later known as Ebonics, also crossed over: words like "*bling*" and "*diss*" have been added to the Oxford English Dictionary.

Women are prominent in Hip-Hop Culture but the arrival of 'Gangsta Rap' in the 1990s, with its themes of violence, drugs and masculine bagging, introduced **misogyny** (hostility to women).

Hip-Hop is now a part of **Global Culture** (p23) and, because it has been adopted by White fans (such as the rapper Eminem) and other ethnic groups, it is **Hybrid Culture** (p26) too.

Research: revisit your notes from **Section A** and add details about **Back** and **Nayak** ('White Wannabes,' p27) and **Brah** (Asian code-switchers, p70); listen to *The Message* (1982) by Grandmaster Flash & the Furious Five and *Rapper's Delight* (1979) by the Sugar Hill Gang to hear the early chart hits of Hip-Hop

RESEARCH PROFILE: CASHMORE (1997)

Ellis Cashmore (*The Black Culture Industry*, 1997) studied the origins of Hip-Hop, beginning in 1960s Jamaica. He traces it to the Bronx and other Black neighbourhoods of New York City in 1970s where mixing decks and a rapping Master of Ceremonies (MC) were features of outdoor block parties. By the 1980s, Rap music was promoted worldwide by big companies. However, Rap is constantly changing and as a result it has been adapted to suit a whole variety of Youth groups. Different cultures adopted Rap and added their own style to it.

Cashmore argues that this sort of **Hybridity** (p26) is a key characteristic of Hip-Hop, making it a truly **Postmodern** music genre and Subculture. However, Cashmore uses case studies of the Motown record label and the careers of Michael Jackson and Prince to argue that Black music has been turned into a **commodity** (a product to be sold) for White-controlled corporations, losing its authenticity and its ability to challenge racial injustice.

More recent critics have complained that commercial Rap music contributes to negative stereotypes of Black youths as criminals, Black women as sex objects and normalising sexism, violence and drug use. Others argue that Rap music is empowering for Black youths facing racism and poverty.

YOUTH SUBCULTURES RELATED TO HYBRIDITY

We have already seen that most Youth Subcultures are **Hybrid Cultures**: Mods and Skinheads both drew on Caribbean musical and fashion influences and White youngsters have embraced Hip-Hop. **Dick Hebdige (1979**, p140**)** claims that **Spectacular Youth Subcultures** can be read **semiologically** as *"responses to the black immigrant presence in Britain."*

Postmodernists argue this hybridity has gone even further with the arrival, since the 1990s, of **Global Culture** (p23) and the Internet. Youth Culture in general is now about 'picking and mixing' stylistic elements from other cultures as well as a 'retro' element of nostalgia. A lot of young people listen to playlists (e.g. on services like Spotify) where pop music from the 1960s sits next to the latest R&B.

Paul Willis (1990) argues that the Spectacular Youth Subcultures are fading because there are so many '**style and taste cultures**' available for young people to define their Identity. Willis argues that young people engage in **symbolic creativity** in the way they adopt fashion and leisure products to create their own unique style. This is similar to **Polhemus'** '**Supermarket of Style**.'

Critics argue that there are *still* Youth Subcultures (e.g. Goths, p127).

Hollands & Chatterton (2002) complain that mainstream Youth Culture is increasingly dominated by **Consumer Culture**, where young people visit corporately owned bars and nightclubs, listen to commercial chart music and dress in high street fashions in a **passive** rather than a creative way. However, there are still 'alternative' and 'authentic' subcultural venues outside the mainstream for young people who go outside the centres of towns and cities (an example would be Makina, *below*).

AO2 ILLUSTRATION: MAKINA

Makina is Spanish hardcore techno music with rapid rap-style MCing that has become 'the sound of the North East of England.' It emerged from clubs like the New Monkey in Sunderland in the 1990s. These venues didn't serve alcohol so young people were allowed in at 16 – although the New Monkey was closed down in 2006 for drug offences there. Makina might be of Spanish origin, but it is rooted in the experiences of the poorest estates in Newcastle, Sunderland and Middlesbrough, with lyrics about partying, stealing cars, being chased by the police and doing drugs, but not the consumerist bragging about fashion labels and the misogyny about women found in Gangsta Rap.

Music journalist **Joe Muggs (2014)** calls Makina *"proper, in-the-foundations-of-the-city, cross-generational folk music"* which means it has an authenticity that commercial pop and R&B don't have as well as being part of the Youth Culture of the North East.

Mark Rimmer (2010) carried out an ethnographic study of Makina fans from a deprived Newcastle housing estate and concludes the music helps them *"help them think through the somewhat contradictory processes at work"* in their community.

Research: listen to Makina music or better still watch *Makina!* **(dir. Aponysus, 2020)**, a 20 minute British Council documentary about the music and the subculture; revisit your notes from **1A: Socialisation, Culture & Identity** and apply **Thornton**'s ideas of **subcultural capital** to this.

RESEARCH PROFILE: MAFFESOLI (1977)

It's an important insight of Postmodernism that Identities like Class become unstable in a fluid postmodern culture. French sociologist **Michel Maffesoli (*The Time of the Tribes*, 1996)** argues that Youth Culture and Subcultures have been replaced by 'urban tribes' or **Neo-Tribes**.

Maffesoli's ideas are explored by **Andy Bennet (*Subcultures or Neo-Tribes?*, 1999)** who studied the Newcastle nightclub scene in the 1990s (including **Makina**, *above*). He found young people didn't define themselves as members of any particular group, mixed and matched musical tastes and shared interests and lifestyle in common rather than social class or values.

Bennet discovered these Neo-Tribes are much more **fluid** than the old Youth Subcultures: a young person could belong to several and drift from one to another. An analogy would be a multi-dancefloor nightclub where young people could go from venues playing Rap to commercial pop to hard rock or retro music, mingling with different people in each environment.

EXAM PRACTICE: YOUTH SUBCULTURES

The OCR exam has three questions in **Paper 1 Section B**. Questions 4-6 are on Families & Relationships and questions 10-12 are on the Media, but this Study Guide is focused on Option 2, which contains questions 7-9:

7. Outline two ways youth subcultures are related to ethnicity. **[12 marks: 8 AO1 + 4 AO2]**

This is very similar to Q2 in Section A, but with no source A and B, so it has to come entirely from your own learning. Notice that the importance of AO1 and AO2 is switched: you get more marks for knowledge of Sociology here and far fewer for real life illustrations.

*Make **two sociological points** about ethnic subcultures – perhaps from a Consensus/assimilation and a Conflict/cultural defence viewpoint. Each point should have its own paragraph and be supported by evidence from a named sociologist or piece of research. You have 10 minutes to write this.*

8. Explain and briefly evaluate the view that youth subcultures are related to hybridity. **[16 marks: 8 AO1 + 4 AO2 + 4 AO3]**

This is similar to Q3 in Section A, but again with fewer marks given to AO2 illustration.

*Write three paragraphs: **two argue in favour** of the question and the **third paragraph argues against** (e.g. that youth subcultures reflect working class identity). For example, you could write about the **Postmodernist** idea of fluidity using Makina as an example, then the argument for **Maffesoli's theory of Neo-Tribes** (p124) but finish with the CCCS' argument that youth cultures are rooted in the experience of growing up working class.*

9. Assess the view that youth subcultures are a form of resistance to Capitalism. **[24 marks: 8 AO1 + 8 AO2 + 8 AO3]**

This is a full essay question, with equal weight given to knowledge of Sociology, illustration and evaluation.

*You need to make **3 points in favour** of the viewpoint in the question (e.g. that youth subcultures resist Capitalism) and **3 opposed** to these neo-Marxist views. The best structure is a point-then-criticism, point-then-criticism and point-then-criticism; no conclusion is required (but it might help). For example, you could write about the CCCS' idea of Spectacular Youth Subcultures like Skinheads resisting Capitalism (but criticise it for being a "magical solution"), then consider Mods or Punks; good criticisms include arguments that these Spectacular Youth Subcultures have faded and been replaced by passive consumers – or never reflected girls or non-White British youths. You have 30 minutes for this essay.*

CHAPTER SEVEN – DEVIANT SUBCULTURES

Deviance is going against the **norms** and/or **values** of society. A similar term is **transgression**, which means more specifically going against the rules or laws.

There has been concern about Youth Deviance since Youth Culture first emerged in the 1950s and the idea that Youth was a period of irrational **'Storm & Stress'** goes back even further (**Hall, 1904**, p97). Some Youth Subcultures seem to take a delight in being transgressive, with shocking fashions, offensive language and celebrating anti-social behaviour.

Positive Views of Youth Deviance

Even if young people are deviant, that might not be a bad thing. Society *needs* a certain level of deviance so that there can be progress and innovation. Young people have to break the rules to come up with new ideas. **Mary Quant**'s miniskirt was shocking when it first appeared in 1963. Over time, if society reacts positively to this deviance, it moves into the mainstream, as can be seen with **Hip-Hop** (p122). This view is associated with **Functionalism**.

A different view is that youth deviance is a justified response to real problems in society. Young people have not yet settled into social roles, they still have ideals and social norms that adults take for granted are seen by the young with fresh eyes. Young people reject society and express this rejection by breaking the rules. Their deviance is an act of **resistance** through symbolic **rituals**, albeit an ultimately ineffective one.

This view is associated with **Conflict Perspectives**, especially **Neo-Marxism**.

Negative Views of Youth Deviance

Even if a small amount of youth deviance benefits society, a lot of it can poison society. Youth Deviance can be self-harming (such as taking drugs and truanting school) and it harms the community (such as vandalising public buildings or intimidating neighbours and shoppers). When youth deviance tips into violence, it can take the form of gang warfare or racist hate, which terrifies and oppresses innocent people. This sort of extreme deviance is a symptom that something is wrong on a deeper level in society.

This view is associated with **Functionalism** and especially the **New Right Perspective** (p129). It used to be rejected by **Marxism**, which interpreted youth deviance in a rather heroic light or else regarded it as **scaremongering and scapegoating** of young people from working class backgrounds. However, **Neo-Marxists** (p131) recognise that not all youth deviance targets Capitalism: other poor people and ethnic minorities are often the victims.

AO2 ILLUSTRATION: GOTHS

Goths are a Youth Subculture that grew out of Punk in the early 1980s. Goths dress in black, often in fashions linked to sexual fetishes (leather, bondage) or 19th century glamour (lace, corsets). White face makeup is popular, with dramatic eye makeup and dyed black hair, often outrageously styled. Body piercing is popular. The overall appearance is related to horror genres, such as vampires and zombies. The subculture embraces melancholy and the dark aspect of life.

Gothic music was pioneered by **Siouxsie & the Banshees** (Siouxsie Sioux established the Gothic look), **Joy Division** and **The Cure**. The music tends to be gloomy with lyrics that explore alienation, mental ill health and suicide as well as horror themes.

Paul Hodkinson (2002) argues that Goths remain a Spectacular Youth Subculture, contrary to theories that these subcultures have declined, and argues that, unlike Punk, members remain part of the subculture long into adulthood.

In 2007, **Sophie Lancaster** and her boyfriend Robert Maltby were attacked in a park by a gang of teenagers because of their Goth appearance. Sophie was murdered. There was a petition to widen the definition of Hate Crime to include attacks on subcultures like Goths.

Goths are a subculture with strongly deviant appearances and interests, but who are not violent or associated with conflict. Membership of the subculture is more like to make you a **_victim_** or violence than a perpetrator.

Research: listen to Goth music; find out more about the murder of Sophie Lancaster.

Goth couple (photo: fluffy_steve)

RESEARCH PROFILE: DURKHEIM (1895)

Emile Durkheim, a Functionalist and founder of Sociology, wrote *The Rules of Sociological Method* **(1895)** in which he describes the **'society of saints'** where everyone is an *"exemplary individual"* and *"crimes are unknown."* Durkheim argues that there will still be *"faults"* among the saints. These faults appear trivial to outsiders but among the saints they cause *"the same scandal that the ordinary offense does in ordinary consciousness."*

Durkheim's insight is that deviance is **relative**. In a society where everyone is well-behaved, then sneezing in public or a mild swear word will bring fierce sanctions. In a society of barbarians or outlaws, no one bothers with sneezing or swearing, but murder or cannibalism will bring the same fierce sanctions. There will always be deviance because there will always be rules that can be broken and how trivial or serious the transgression is depends on how well-behaved everyone else is.

PERSPECTIVES ON YOUTH DEVIANCE

Perspectives are very broad viewpoints but they tend to fall into the camps outlined above, either seeing youth deviance as necessary/admirable or as a danger.

CONSENSUS PERSPECTIVE: FUNCTIONALISM

Functionalists believe in the importance of value consensus in society, which is reinforced is through **policing the margins**: agencies of social control reward those who conform or punish those who deviate. Shared disapproval of deviance actually strengthens social solidarity.

Kingsley Davies (1967) suggests deviance acts as a safety valve for society. By engaging in deviance, people 'let off steam' and can return to their respectable lives.

Davies gives the example of prostitution, suggesting that visiting prostitutes makes it easier for men to stay married. This argument isn't just weird and out-of-date: it shows a problem with Functionalism, that it is prepared to make excuses for social evils if they are somehow 'in the common good.'

The isolation people experience in Capitalist societies increases deviance. Rapid change increased deviance because of **anomie**: the collapse of social control and social solidarity. Young people are particularly isolated, so their subcultures are more likely to be deviant.

Many people criticise the idea that deviance is normal and functional. Crime is a serious problem for victims and for society and we should be trying to prevent crime, not excuse it. **Feminists** object to the idea that the exploitation or abuse of women is made acceptable if it helps society function.

Marxists argue that laws are made by the state and work in the interests of the ruling class. Instead of value consensus, they argue there is **ideology** or **hegemony** supporting capitalism.

Traditional Functionalism does not consider why some people commit crime and others do not. Most people do not commit crime.

The New Right

The New Right could be considered a 'spin-off' from Functionalism in the 1980s. Its central assumption is that the vital value consensus has either collapsed or is about to collapse, so emergency measures are needed to restore it.

The New Right diagnoses the core institution for value consensus as the nuclear family (married parents and their children) and the biggest threat to this as the **Welfare State**. The Welfare State is the political arrangement that pays benefits to the poor and the unemployed.

Critics of the Welfare State argue it **rewards worklessness** and **undermines the family** (since couples are not forced to stay together for monetary reasons if the state pays for their children).The lone parent family (especially the single mother with children) is a focus for the New Right, who argue that lone parents cannot effectively **socialise** their children, who grow up 'feral': the girls get pregnant without marrying and live on child benefits, repeating the cycle; the boys search for a father-figure and join **gangs**.

The New Right identifies a **'benefits trap'** that means unemployed people would end up worse off if they took a job, creating an incentive to stay unemployed and leading to **generational unemployment**, where families have parents and grandparents who do not work and claim benefits. The solution is to cut back benefits, forcing healthy adults to find work and take responsibility for their families.

*These are controversial arguments. Many people (including but not limited to **Marxists**) would argue that unemployed people desperately want to work. The decline of British industry in the 1970s and '80s mean that there isn't work to find in some deprived communities and the rise of the 'gig economy' means such work as can be found won't support a family.*

One of the main speakers for the New Right is American sociologist **Charles Murray (1984)**, who warns that the benefits trap and the collapse of the nuclear family has created an **'underclass.'** The underclass is made up of lone parent families on benefits, where the mothers cannot control their children and fathers avoid their responsibilities, living a life of petty crime.

Research: revisit your notes on **Section A** and link these ideas to **Charles Murray** (p57) and **social control in the workforce** (55) – including the arguments by the **Joseph Rowntree Foundation (2012)** and **Macmillan (2011)** that cast doubt on the existence of Murray's underclass.

Culture & Identity

Functionalism has produced another spin-off called **Subcultural Theory** to explain deviant subcultures. Some focus on how some young people experience frustration in their attempts to be successful at school and respond by forming an **Anti-School Subculture** (p139).

A different approach comes from **Walter B Miller (1958)** who argues that 'lower class' people already exist in a subculture which has distinctive values that are different from the mainstream. He calls these subcultural values **'Focal Concerns'** and they include things like **Excitement** (needing short term thrills) and **Toughness** (needing to prove your strength to others). An interesting Focal Concern is **Fatalism**: believing nothing you can do will change what's going to happen so there's no point in trying. Middle class children are supposedly raised with the belief that they can decide their own future, which is why they embrace **Meritocracy** (p60).

These Focal Concerns don't automatically make a working-class youth deviant, but they make it more likely, especially when they are strongly **internalised** through **socialisation** to form a **Deviant Identity**.

Miller's ideas are rather vague: just who exactly are the 'lower classes' and how do you measure Focal Concerns? Some would say Miller is just recycling snobby prejudices about the poor.

This Subcultural Theory is criticised for ignoring girls and applying mainly to White boys. More importantly, it seems to give up a very important principle of Functionalism, which is that there is **value consensus** in society. It implies that the working classes are a separate culture in conflict with middle class culture and this is an idea that you normally find in **Marxism**.

CONFLICT PERSPECTIVE: MARXISM

Marxists don't accept that deviance comes from being badly socialised and they certainly don't agree that there's something inherently deviant about being working class.

Instead, Marxists argue that Capitalism itself is **criminogenic** – it is a system that creates crime and drives people to commit crime. **Young (1984**, p42**)** claims we live in a 'bulimic society' where the constant need to get the latest products, brands and fashions causes people to become deranged.

For Marxists, the real criminals are the rulers of the Capitalist system and they argue that the **White Collar Crime** carried out by corporations does far more damage to society than muggers or hooligans on the streets.

However, **ruling class ideology** (especially as it is presented through the **Media**) causes people to focus on the wrong things. People have an exaggerated fear of street crime and working-class youths, but dismiss white collar crime as harmless or unimportant. The police crack down on working class youths, but don't pursue white collar criminals; this is called **selective enforcement**.

This can be explained by **Althusser (1970**, p51**)** who identifies the **Ideological State Apparatus (ISA**, e.g. the Media) and the **Repressive State Apparatus (RSA**, e.g. the police) which combine to support Capitalism.

Research: revisit your notes on **Section A** and link these ideas to **Jock Young, Edwin Sutherland** (p49) and **Louis Althusser**.

Neo-Marxism

Neo means 'new' and Neo-Marxism emerged in the 1970s as update of Marxist thought. A big inspiration was **Antonio Gramsci (1891-1937)** who moved away from the idea of a revolution to overthrow Capitalism. Gramsci observed that the ruling class was no longer a literal class of aristocrats and factory owners, but had become a **Hegemony**, a confederation of influential people with a vested interest in keeping Capitalism going. Gramsci pointed out that Hegemony **'manufactures consent'** through education and the Media.

The **CCCS** (p113) developed Neo-Marxism in books like *Resistance Through Rituals* **(1975)**. Youth Subcultures are only 'deviant' in hegemonic terms – they are presented that way by the Media in order to make them seem like the real enemy. In fact, working class youths are engaged in a **counter-hegemonic struggle**. Since they cannot literally tear down Capitalism, they do so symbolically, through **'rituals'** like **Punk** music (p140) or **Skinhead** fashions (p119).

A key member of the CCCS is **Stuart Hall** who wrote *Policing The Crisis* **(1978)** at a time when the UK was rocked by strikes and suffering mass unemployment. Hall points out that the British newspapers started a **moral panic** (p148) about **Black muggers** at a time when there was a genuine chance of Capitalism collapsing. This distracted people from the crisis, inflamed hostility between the White and Black working classes and justified police crackdowns.

This is termed the **'divide & rule'** approach to Hegemonic control: make the non-hegemonic groups (the White and Black working classes) hostile to each other so they never unite to challenge hegemonic power. The White working class welcome the deployment of heavy policing, because they believe (wrongly) it is protecting them. Hall claims this is **manufacture of consent** in action.

*Hall (and notice this Hall is not the same as G Stanley Hall who coined 'Storm & Stress') wrote an absolute classic with **Policing The Crisis** but has been attacked for creating a **conspiracy theory** since it's not clear exactly how the newspapers united in this way. Moreover, negative stereotypes against the Black working classes existed before and continued after the 'Crisis.'*

Neo-Marxism has been influential in Left Wing politics. It paints a more complex picture than the hard-done-by Proletariat rising up against the wealthy Bourgeoisie who want to keep them down-trodden. Instead, there is a struggle going on at every level of society between different groups and ideas and this struggle is often symbolic. This insight leads to **Intersectionality** (p63) which focuses on a plurality of privileged and oppressed identities and views language itself as a force for oppression.

Culture & Identity

The work of the CCCS is sometimes termed '**Marxist Subcultural Theory**.' It assumes that most adults find it hard to resist **hegemonic control** because they are trapped by family responsibilities and careers. Young people are not yet trapped: they don't have family responsibilities; they might only work part-time or be unemployed. They are more able to **resist** hegemony.

Each generation of working-class youth faces similar problems but in different social and cultural circumstances. Each group adopts a style (dress, speech, music, behaviour) based on their circumstances and expresses their **resistance** through this style. **Mods** reflect the circumstances of the 1960s by displaying their (small) wealth through sharp suits and Mary Quant fashions; **Punks** reflect the 1970s by displaying their contempt for conventional values.

The Punk band The Sex Pistols famously used the F-word on live TV in 1976, triggering mass complaints.

Mike Brake (1980) calls these 'magical solutions' because they do not really change the way society is structured. But they are meaningful to the members of the subculture as part of their Identity.

Marxist Subcultural Theory is challenged by pointing out that it only focuses on resistance and it ignores subcultures like **Geeks** (p26) who are quite conservative and embrace **Consumer Culture** (although often an obscure part of consumer culture, e.g. comics). Similarly, it doesn't pay enough attention to how Youth Subcultures are **manipulated** by advertisers and businesses.

Finally, it can be accused of glamorising Youth Subcultures as heroic underdogs, when some of these youths are violent and racist criminals.

CONFLICT PERSPECTIVE: FEMINISM

In the past, youth deviance was seen as a problem with young males and most of the attention of sociologists have gone into forms of male deviance like gangs and violence. Feminists point out this is a male-centred (**androcentric**) bias in Sociology and McRobbie & Garber identify this bias in the work of the CCCS (p30).

However, young females are deviant too and there is evidence that teenage girls start deviant behaviour younger than teenage boys (engaging in shoplifting or drug-use) and that the rates of deviance for males and females are becoming more similar.

Freda Adler (1975) predicted this with her **Liberation Thesis**, claiming that, as young women increasingly faced the same sort of pressures as young men to get qualifications, jobs and public recognition, they would have the same opportunities and temptations to engage in deviancy.

Some Feminists think the rates of female deviancy might be under-reported. The **Chivalry Thesis** claims that police and judges 'go easy' on women, especially if they show remorse (e.g. by crying). This links to **Labelling Theory**, since young males are labelled as deviant but girls are not.

Culture & Identity

In **Section A**, you learned about **the 'Ladette' subculture of the 1990s** (p74). Ladettes were teenage girls or women in their early twenties with a lifestyle of drinking and drug-taking, violence, swearing and law-breaking. The shocking behaviour of 'Ladettes' was a common feature of news reporting in the late 1990s and early 2000s.

Ladettes seem to support Adler's Liberation Thesis: as males and females become more equal, females start to show the same sorts of behaviour that has been normal for males for a long time. **Angela Smith (2013)** argues that "*the 'ladette' liberated young women from the confines of a very conservative form of femininity because they could behave just like men.*"

Other Feminists focus instead on how young girls are socialised into being compliant and conforming. **Ann Oakley (1982)** explains how girls are socialised in a different way from boys, with a focus on beauty and submission, rather than risk-taking behaviour and aggression.

According to this view, women are *not* equal to men or experiencing liberation. These Feminists regard the brief 'Ladette' subculture as a **moral panic** created by the newspapers (p150).

The actual purpose of the moral panic was to lead a backlash *against* liberated women and force traditional and conforming gender identities on them (similar to the view of **Susan Faludi in Section A,** p75).

The focus on female deviance is often used to justify male deviance. Feminists argue that an important part of '**rape culture**' is the idea that women who get drunk in public or dress in a sexually provocative way are encouraging men to abuse them. This is '**victim-blaming**' and **McRobbie & Garber** noticed it applied to the female members of Spectacular Youth Subcultures like the **female Mods** (p120).

SOCIAL ACTION PERSPECTIVE: INTERACTIONISM

The Interactionist Perspective sees young people as negotiating their Identity through a series of interactions with their peers, their parents and the state.

David Matza (1964) suggests **Drift Theory**. He argues that there aren't really any deviant Youth Subcultures. All groups in society share **subterranean values**: deviant urges to go against social norms, such as partying hard, drinking, swearing, fighting or having sex with the wrong people. We keep these urges under control and act on conventional values, but indulge these urges at leisure times (weekends, holidays abroad). We 'drift' between conforming and deviant behaviour. **Restraining your subterranean values** and **indulge them safely** is a learned skill, so young people are more likely to do it inappropriately, at the wrong time, in the wrong place.

Culture & Identity

Edwin Lemert (1967) points out a distinction between **primary and secondary deviance**.

Primary deviance is something everybody does: we've all stolen things (if only pens from the office or towels from the hotel), broken the law, damaged things that don't belonged to us, had romantic interactions with someone we shouldn't, used obscene language or been violent. Most of the time it goes unnoticed and there are no consequences.

Secondary deviance is deviance that society reacts to. Someone 'calls it out' and assigns a label: we are blamed, accused; people are shocked; the authorities step in. This includes being labelled as a criminal (or a 'thug' or a 'punk' or a 'slut'). At first this label doesn't conform to our self-image and that leads to anxiety. Eventually, we alter our self-image to conform to the label: this is the **Self-Fulfilling Prophecy (SFP)**.

Some labels have **Master Status** and are particularly hard to negotiate or remove. If you are labelled as 'lazy' you can negotiate that label (*I'm only lazy with subjects I don't enjoy*) or prove it wrong. If you are labelled as a criminal. It's hard to negotiate (it's no good saying you're not a criminal because you only steal from rich people) or remove – the label can stick for years.

Entire Subcultures can be labelled as 'deviant' as a group. If you imitate Punk fashions, you acquire secondary deviance, a deviant label that you cannot negotiate and you might end up becoming the violent thug society expects you to be.

Since young people have less power in society, it's harder for them to avoid secondary deviance or negotiate deviant labels. This is why they get deviant labels more than adults.

Critics say that secondary deviance is only a good explanation of delinquency and non-serious crime; it's hard to argue that murder is only regarded as deviant because society labels it that way. It's also hard to see how labelling can explain hidden crimes like child abuse.

Research: revisit your notes on **Section A** and link these ideas to **Howard Becker** (p68)

YOUTH DEVIANCE: A TOOLKIT

You need to know about four specific types of deviant Youth Subcultures and some of the statistical trends about youth deviance in UK society.

DELINQUENT SUBCULTURES

Delinquency is a term for youth deviance: the sort of antisocial behaviour that teenagers get up to which falls short of being criminal or counts as **petty crime** (non-serious crime). Examples include truanting, under-age drinking and smoking, swearing, fighting, shoplifting and joyriding (stealing a car, driving it for fun then abandoning it).

Matza's Drift Theory (p133) and **Miller's Focal Concerns** (p130) are good explanations (up to a point) of delinquent subcultures. Most youths grow out of delinquent behaviour, although Matza points out that adults carry on expressing subterranean values, but less publicly. **Chambliss' study of the Saints & the Roughnecks** (p110) is a good account of delinquency linked to **labelling**.

AO2 ILLUSTRATION: TEDDY BOYS

Teddy Boys – or Teds – were Britain's first Youth Subculture from the 1950s. They came to public attention after the film *Rock Around the Clock* (1956) arrived in British cinemas: young Teds rioted in the cinemas, slashing seats and throwing bottles, then fought with the police in the street. The newspapers started a **moral panic** (p148) about the 'teen menace.'

Teddy Boys were also involved in the **1958 Notting Hill Race Riots**.

Teddy Boys wore velvet jackets, suede shoes (known as brothel-creepers or beetle-crushers) and bootlace ties. They greased their hair and styled it with fringes called quiffs. The clothing was based on Edwardian fashion (1901-1910) mixed with American influences (like the ties) because of their love of American rock'n'roll.

They also listened to Black American music like jazz and blues; similar to **Skinheads** (p119), they loved Black music but were hostile to Black immigrants who were arriving in Britain as part of the **Windrush Generation**.

Teddy Girls (also called Judies) wore the same long jackets, pencil skirts or rolled-up jeans and hair in ponytails. The glamorous look was a rejection of post-War 'Austerity' – in the UK at this time, clothing was expensive and fashions were monotonous and drab for ordinary people.

Research: *Rock Around the Clock*; Windrush Generation; 1958 Notting Hill riots; post-War Austerity

RESEARCH PROFILE: JEFFERSON (1976)

Tony Jefferson (*Resistance Through Rituals*, 1976) uses **Neo-Marxist semiology** (p131) to argue that jackets worn by Teds were a subversion of the Edwardian 'Dandy' style.

Jefferson argues that Teds were extremely sensitive about their lower-class status and wore (old fashioned) high class clothing to give themselves glamour and a sense of privilege.

Jefferson uses semiology to explain that the working class Teds took codes that had previously been understood as high class (the expensive velvet coats) and gave them a new working class meaning: he calls it the **'proletarianisation'** of upper class styles. Jeffersom argues this insecurity or "over-sensitivity" about their high-class aspiration vs their lower class status explains the violence of the Ted Subculture.

CRIMINAL SUBCULTURES

A criminal subculture is more organised than a delinquent one; delinquents might commit petty crime but criminal subcultures are focused on serious crime like drug-dealing, theft or extortion (taking money by threats).

AO2 ILLUSTRATION: YARDIES & RUDEBOYS

The first Caribbean immigrants to the UK in the 1950s were sometimes nicknamed 'yardies' and they contributed a lot to British culture, especially in music, but were mostly working-age adults looking for jobs. Back in Jamaica, in poverty-stricken Trenchtown, violent street gangs emerged in the 1970s, also known as Yardies or Posses.

A government crackdown in the '80s meant some of these Yardies migrated to the UK. Yardies have been linked to gun crime and dealing in marijuana and crack cocaine.

Some critics suggest Yardies are a Media-driven **moral panic** (p148) and not a real criminal subculture at all.

Yardies are not a Spectacular Youth Subculture (p139) but have some links to the Caribbean Rudeboy Subculture of the 1960s. Rudeboys listened to ska and rocksteady music – and later reggae – and wore sharp suits and pork pie or trilby hats. They influenced the tastes of **Mods** (p120) and **Skinheads** (p119). 'Rudeboy' has become a part of 21st century urban slang and a greeting.

Research: Yardies and the 1993 murder of PC Patrick Dunne; Rudeboys; listen to rocksteady, ska and reggae music

RESEARCH PROFILE: CLOWARD & OHLIN (1960)

Cloward & Ohlin are Functionalists who argue that, alongside the **legitimate opportunity structure** (school, jobs, careers – the **Meritocracy**, p60), there is an **illegitimate opportunity structure** (a career in crime). Just as not all people can access the legitimate opportunity structure (because of poor qualifications, unemployment, etc.), the illegitimate opportunity structures aren't available to everyone either.

Cloward & Ohlin identify three illegitimate opportunity structures: **(1) Criminal**, which is organised, like the Mafia, with a 'career path' for young recruits that mirrors the legitimate meritocratic structures (bonuses for good work, promotions, etc.); **(2) Conflict**, where gangs compete over territory ("turf wars"), which is violent and only occasional lucrative (some money from drugs or theft); **(3) Retreatist**, where groups who cannot join organised crime or gangs simply 'drop out' and become drug addicts.

Cloward & Ohlin's ideas have been criticised, because the three types frequently blur together; for example, many people say Yardies are not an organised Criminal structure but a disorganised Conflict structure. All three types might use drugs and fight over turf.

Like most Functionalist theories, Cloward & Ohlin don't explore *why* working class males are denied access to legitimate opportunities or why only a minority of working class males join these illegitimate opportunity structures instead. They don't explain why women, who are also denied opportunities, aren't more involved in crime.

GANG SUBCULTURES

A gang is any group of young people who socialise together support each other; many of these gangs are perfectly law-abiding. Socialists are more interested in deviant gangs who cause trouble in the community.

Cloward & Ohlin define a gang as a **Conflict Subculture** that is less organised than a **Criminal Subculture**. Gangs could be seen as a midway point between loosely organised **Delinquent Subcultures** and professionally organised criminal ones. Gangs have rules for admittance, a loose hierarchy (or at least a leader) and usually have membership rituals, a uniform and a name.

AO2 ILLUSTRATION: *COMANDO VERMELHO*

Comando Vermelho (Red Commando) is the oldest Brazilian gang based in a favela named Antares on the outskirts of Rio De Janeiro. It was formed in the 1970s by a mixture of convicts and Communist activists, although it has lost its political identity. In the early 2000s, it fought several small-scale conflicts with the rival gang *Terceiro Comando* but went on to fight a battle with the police in 2007 where 27 people died.

The favelas are slums built around Rio De Janeiro, largely controlled by gangs. *Comando Vermelho* recruits young recruits by sponsoring sports and music events. Brazilian *funk* is a style of music and the gang funds music studio to produce and sell songs and play them on pirate radio stations. The songs advertise the gang and celebrate its dead members.

Comando Vermelho doesn't have a strict hierarchy; it's made up of cells, each with its own leader. In some ways it is more like a criminal organisation than a gang; in other ways, it resembles a private army.

Research: Watch the film *City of God* (dir. Meirelles & Lund, 2002) or *Ross Kemp On Gangs* (*Rio De Janeiro*, 2005), both of which feature Comando Vermelho; research more about the favellas and the gangs there

RESEARCH PROFILE: PATRICK (1973)

James Patrick (a pseudonym, not his real name) is a Scottish sociologist who, in 1966 and aged 23, infiltrated the **Young Team**, a street gang in Maryhill, Glasgow. Patrick had befriended a gang leader, Tim Molloy (also not his real name) who vouched for him to the rest of the gang and protected Patrick's identity. Molloy was the **gatekeeper** who provided **access** for the researcher.

Patrick dressed in the style of the gang (with the top button of his jacket fastened) but did not carry a knife as the others did. He only pretended to take drugs when they did.

Patrick spent 4 months with the gang, meeting the 12 times and making 120 hours of observations. He held back when the Young Team had a fight with the rival Barnes Road Gang. This aroused the suspicions of Dave, another gang member. Although Tim tried to protect him, Patrick ended the research and left the gang before a fight with Dave became inevitable.

Patrick wrote up all his notes from memory afterwards. He published them as *A Glasgow Gang Observed* (1973). He delayed publishing to protect the safety of gang members like Tim from reprisals. He never revealed his own identity to protect himself from the gang seeking revenge for betraying their trust.

The research demonstrates the violence of gangs and also their loose hierarchical structure and precise dress codes.

*Patrick's study is a **participant observation**, where he joined the group he was studying and took part in its activities. It is a **covert observation** because the other members did not realise Patrick was observing them. These concepts will be important when you study **2A: Research Methods**.*

ANTI-SCHOOL SUBCULTURES

A deviant subculture that falls short of delinquency (but sometimes overlaps with it) is the Anti-School Subculture. This is a sub-group of teenagers who reject educational attainment as a goal. They might truant from school and, in classes, disrupt lessons or simply refuse to work. These students are not deterred by school punishments and may even take some pride in being punished.

Outside of school, these young people may or may not be **delinquent** or involved in Criminal Subcultures. Many are perfectly well-behaved outside of school: they want to work and earn money, but not sit exams and do homework.

Playing truant on the Thames (photo: pily pily)

AO2 ILLUSTRATION: TRUANTING

Officially, the unexcused absence rate in all schools in England is around 1.4%. This amounts to two and half days during the academic year. However, the charity **Family Lives** estimates 64,000 pupils skip school every day and not all of these get recorded as unauthorised. The 1996 Education Act means parents pay a £60 fine if their child truants and a court can impose a £2,500 fine for persistent truanting. Only 13% of persistent truants achieved 5+ GCSEs at level 4+ compared to 60% among non-truants. Persistent absenteeism has also been linked to crime, teenage pregnancy and drug abuse. Truants are more likely to suffer from unemployment and social isolation: *"Children who miss school, miss out as adults"* (**Nick Gibb, 2012**).

Ensuring young people stay in school is important for social order, both because they are less able to carry out crime or delinquency right now and they're less likely to have social problems for years afterwards. However, young people sometimes miss school to escape bullying, because they need to work or because they are carers at home. Not all truanting is linked to poverty: in 2016, Bath & North East Somerset had one of the highest levels of truancy despite being one of the wealthiest districts.

RESEARCH PROFILE: COHEN (1955)

Albert Cohen (don't confuse him with Stan Cohen, p147) wrote ***Delinquent Boys* (1955)**. Cohen is a Functionalist who thinks that everyone learns the same values through socialisation, so working class youths have the same goals in life as middle-class youths.

Cohen argues that students always seek **status** (respect, praise, success). Working-class students cannot compete with their middle-class peers. They experience **status frustration**. Rather than accept their inferior status, they form a deviant subculture which 'flips' mainstream norms and values. This means things that were good (like handing in homework and following the rules) become 'bad' and things that were bad (like destroying school property and getting punished by teachers) become 'good.' Now the anti-school students have status in their own eyes.

In some ways this is like **Miller**'s **Focal Concerns** (p130), but Cohen insists the deviant working class youths start off socialised into society's **value consensus**, but then they rebel against it.

Paul Willis' study of 'the Lads' (p41) is in opposition to Cohen's ideas. Willis claims that 'the Lads' never had any interest in 'becoming middle-class' or succeeding at school. They weren't 'frustrated' because education never offered them anything they cared about.

Cohen only discusses boys (a problem shared by many **Neo-Marxists** who criticise his ideas) and fails to address the inequalities of the wider Capitalist society working class boys live in.

SPECTACULAR YOUTH SUBCULTURES

This is a term used by sociologists to describe some of the British Youth Subcultures of the 1950s, '60 and '70s, including **Teddy Boys** (p134), **Mods** (p120), **Skinheads** (p119) and **Punks**. These subcultures were visually distinctive in the way they dressed and confrontational in their attitudes to outsiders. They were associated with music genres that inspired them. **Goths** (p127) would also count as a Spectacular Youth Subculture that emerged in the 1980s but they are less political and working class than the earlier subcultures.

Punks (photo: agogo)

AO2 ILLUSTRATION: PUNKS (continued from p53)

Punk appeared in the late 1970s. Punks adopted a shocking look, with brightly coloured hair shaved or shaped into spikes or fins; makeup was aggressive, often with facial piercings; clothing was torn leather, denim and plastic, often recycled from second-hand items. Punk celebrated anti-authority, do-it-yourself values.

There was cross-dressing among Punks, such as men wearing ripped-up skirts, fishnet tights and excessive makeup, or women with shaved heads wearing denim jackets and combat boots. This made Punk popular with young women, despite its values of masculine strength and anger.

Punk music (typified by **The Sex Pistols**) celebrated anarchy, causing offence and aggression. During the Queen's Silver Jubilee in 1977, the Six Pistols had a Number 1 hit with their mocking version of *God Save The Queen*, which was banned by the BBC for comparing the royal family to *"a fascist regime."*

RESEARCH PROFILE: HEBDIGE (1979, continued from p53

Dick Hebdige studied Punks as part of the **CCCS** (p113) and wrote *Subculture: The Meaning of Style* **(1979)**. Hebdige used the term **'bricolage'** to describe Punk culture, referring to the way it found new uses for old objects, giving them new meaning, such as dresses made from bin liners and piercings from safety pins. Punks often combined these with unexpected objects such as sexual bondage gear and swastikas. Hebdige argues that punks set out deliberately to shock mainstream society.

Hebdige argues that all subcultures develop in a similar way: (1) they form out of **resistance** to hegemony, (2) mainstream society sees these groups as deviant, leading to **fear and anxiety** about them, (3) this increases the **subculture's resistant power** but only temporarily, (4) **incorporation**, which is when business **commodify** the style of the subculture (turn it into a product for anyone to buy), (5) the subculture's fashion and music become available to the **mainstream** in a safe non-threatening form (as part of **Consumer Culture**, p21), (6) the **resistant power** of the subculture begins to **die**.

Hebdige explains the 'life cycle' of Punk but he is criticised for ignoring American Punk, which started earlier than the UK scene and lasted longer, with different values and not related to the UK class system.

Research: revisit your notes on **Section A** (e.g. p53) and combine these ideas with the details on Punk as part of **social control**

PATTERNS & TRENDS

According to the **Joseph Rowntree Foundation (JRF)** more than 4/10 males and 1/10 females are likely to be found guilty or cautioned for an offence at some point during their lives. However, only about 5% of males are **chronic offenders** who account for about half of all known offending. The pattern of lifelong offending seems to begin in youth.

According to the **Ministry of Justice (2019)** the number of children who received a caution or sentence has fallen by 83% over the last ten years.

PATTERNS & TRENDS: SOCIAL CLASS

Working class youths have been stereotyped as deviant and criminal for a long time, but what is the truth behind this?

According to **National Prison Survey (2020)**, 41% of male convicts come from unskilled or skilled manual classes. According to the **Mayor of London's Office (2019)**, three-quarters of the boroughs in London with the highest levels of violent offending are also in the top 10 most deprived, while the same boroughs also have higher proportions of children living in poverty than the London average. This certainly links youth crime to deprivation and low social class.

The Prison Reform Trust (2010) reports that 2000-3000 children are in custody at any time. A survey of 200 young people in custody found half came from deprived backgrounds and three-quarters had absent fathers; another common factor was exclusion from school or regular **truanting** (p47). This suggests the issue is more complicated than just 'social class,' with several factors combining to draw youngsters into crime.

However, these **patterns** can be misleading. Prison surveys only include people caught and convicted and given prison sentences; youths from wealthier and better educated backgrounds are more likely to escape detection because their families are more able to afford good lawyers.

Chambliss' Saints & Roughnecks study (p19) shows that children from middle class backgrounds are treated differently by the agencies of social control, are less likely to be labelled negatively and can get away with offences that poorer people cannot. The **Everyone's Invited website** (p40) shows that (sexual) deviancy is widespread at top UK private schools.

This also links to working class youths spending more time on the streets, making their deviance more 'visible' than middle class youth deviance. However, **Smith et al. (2005)** proposes that working class youths do in fact have a more adversarial (conflict) relationship with the police and enjoy risk-taking and 'thumbing their noses' at authority, which makes them more likely to be arrested than just given a warning.

The sociologists of the **New Right** (p38) argue that, within the largely law-abiding working class, there is an **underclass** where the youths are poorly socialised, raised without fathers and involved in crime and gangs from an early age. They claim this underclass accounts for the hard core of working class youth deviancy and a **trend** for the underclass to grow, leading to rising youth deviancy. Other commentators from the **Consensus Perspective** link a **trend** for rising youth deviancy to violent video games, rap lyrics or Internet pornography.

AO2 ILLUSTRATION: THE 2011 LONDON RIOTS

In the summer of 2011, there was a week of rioting in towns and cities across England, but largely in London and starting in Tottenham. TV viewers were shocked to see battles with the police, the burning of cars, buses and shops as well as looting on a huge scale. There were 5 deaths and over £200 million in property damage.

The police made over 3000 arrests and courts had to open for extended hours to process all the cases. An instruction came from the Conservative Government that all rioters be punished with strong sentences, including 4 years for a man who stayed home but encouraged rioting via *Facebook*.

While 12% of the working-age population of the UK are on benefits of some sort, 35% of the adults prosecuted after the riots were on benefits. Some commentators took this as evidence for the link between class and crime – or for the **New Right**'s idea of the crime-prone **underclass**.

London riots (photo: StuartBannock)

PATTERNS & TRENDS: GENDER

There is a stereotype that youth deviancy is linked to males, with young women being better behaved, but is there any basis to this?

According to the **Ministry of Justice (2019)**, 85% of children receiving a caution or a sentence were boys (51% of the population), but girls accounted for 15% (49% of the population).

This certainly supports the idea that males are more deviant and criminal then females. It is tied to the **Feminist** observation that young women experience more **social control** and have to enact their resistance as part of **bedroom culture** (p30) rather than in public, which would explain why they are not arrested by the police. Young males are socialised into risk-taking behaviour as a way of asserting their masculinity; young females are not socialised into asserting their femininity in this way.

A different argument is **Chivalry Theory**, which suggests that, because girls are stereotyped as more fragile and innocent than boys, they are more likely to be ignored, released or let of with warnings rather than arrested, particularly if they show remorse (e.g. by crying).

The Youth Justice Board (2009) shows that the peak age for female offending is 15, but it is 18 for males. This suggests that females start deviant behaviour earlier (but perhaps with less serious transgressions) then grow out of it, whereas male deviance continues into their 20s with much more serious consequences.

There was a concern in the late 1990s that young women were imitating male deviancy, through binge-drinking and violence. In **Socialisation, Culture & Identity** you learned about the **'Ladettes'** and the debate about whether this was a social problem, an example of growing gender equality or a moral panic (see **Chapter 8**) produced by the newspapers to keep young women 'in their place.' However, the Ladette subculture seems to have declined (if it ever existed in the first place) and youth deviancy among girls seems to be limited to bullying, shoplifting and buying stolen goods, whereas male youth deviancy involves fighting and criminal damage (**Campbell et al, 2000**).

However, there does seem to be a **trend** towards more female crime (sometimes called **'pink collar crime'**). In the UK, female arrests increased by 50% in some parts of the UK after a crackdown on petty crime (source: **Prison Reform Trust, 2017**) which supports the Chivalry Theory. Worldwide, the number of women in prison as increased by more than half since 2000 (source: **Institute for Criminal Policy Research, 2017**). This is linked to increasing gender equality, with women having the same opportunities to carry out crimes that men have always had.

AO2 ILLUSTRATION: THE 2011 LONDON RIOTS (cont'd)

While 49% of the population of the UK in 2011 was male, 90% of the adults prosecuted after the riots were male. Some commentators took this as evidence for the link between males and crime.

PATTERNS & TRENDS: ETHNICITY

There are racist stereotypes that youths from some ethnic minorities are more likely to be deviant. According to the **Ministry of Justice (2019)**, 69% of arrests of 10-17 year olds were of White children (84% of the population), arrests of Black children accounted for 16% (5% of the population), arrests of Asian children made up 6% of the total (9% of the population). This shows that, as a proportion of the population, more Black young people are being arrested, but less White youths. However, it should be noted that arrest rates have been falling for *all* ethnic groups over the last 10 years, but for White youths the fall has been faster, widening this gap.

These official figures need to be considered in the light of accusations of **institutional or systemic racism** (*c.f.* **1A: Socialisation, Culture & Identity**). The police might be more likely to stop and search Black youths, more likely to arrest them if they see something suspicious and courts might be more likely to convict them of offences. **Geoff Pearson & Mike Rowe (2020)** spent 7 years observing UK police officers carrying out stop & search and conclude it is overused with Black suspects, which might explain the higher arrest rates for Black youths.

The idea of **secondary deviance** (p42) and **Hall's study of racist moral panics in the news** (p40) should remind you that witnesses might interpret Black youths as behaving suspiciously and be more likely to call the police than they would be for White youths doing the same things.

RESEARCH PROFILE: MAC AN GHAILL (1988)

Mairtin Mac An Ghaill carried out participant observations of his students while working as a teacher in inner city schools the 1980s and reported his findings in *Young, Gifted and Black* **(1988)** – *the title comes from a soul song by Nina Simone.* Mac An Ghaill studies relations between White teachers and two groups of male students with **anti-school subcultures** (pX) whom he terms the (Asian) **Warriors** and the (African-Caribbean) **Rasta Heads**. The Rasta Heads were rebellious but the Warriors more passive. Mac An Ghaill links this to racism in the school system, which alienates both groups but **labels** the Rasta Heads as deviant while treating the Asian students as if they were 'invisible.'

Tony Sewell (*Black Masculinities*, 1997) has a different interpretation. He links the deviant behaviour of Black boys in UK schools to a subculture of **'hyper-masculinity'** due to growing up without a father. In the UK the Black ethnic group has the highest proportion of lone parent households (13% at the 2011 Census). This is a **Functionalist/New Right** argument against Mac An Ghaill's **Neo-Marxist** view of ethnic minority deviance as resistance to racism.

Mac An Ghaill also studied a group of African-Caribbean and Asian female students he termed the **Black Sisters**. The girls also experienced racism in the school system but were more focused on supporting each other and getting qualifications out of the system rather than rebelling against it. This makes Mac An Ghaill's study useful for analysing both ethnicity and gender.

AO2 ILLUSTRATION: THE 2011 LONDON RIOTS (cont'd)

While 3% of the population of the UK in 2011 was Black – rising to 11% in London as a whole – 50% of the adults prosecuted after the riots were Black. Some commentators took this as evidence for the link between ethnicity and crime – or for the **Neo-Marxist** idea of the police targeting Black working class people disproportionately.

EXAM PRACTICE: DEVIANT SUBCULTURES

7. Outline two types of deviant youth subculture. **[12 marks: 8 AO1 + 4 AO2]**

This is very similar to Q2 in Section A, but with no source A and B, so it has to come entirely from your own learning. Notice that the importance of AO1 and AO2 is switched: you get more marks for knowledge of Sociology here and far fewer for real life illustrations.

*Make **two sociological points** about youth deviance – perhaps anti-school and spectacular or else gangs and criminals. Each point should have its own paragraph and be supported by evidence from a named sociologist or piece of research. You have 10 minutes to write this.*

8. Explain and briefly evaluate the view that youth deviance is related to gender. **[16 marks: 8 AO1 + 4 AO2 + 4 AO3]**

This is similar to Q3 in Section A, but again with fewer marks given to AO2 illustration.

*Write three paragraphs: **two argue in favour** of the question and the **third paragraph argues against** (e.g. that youth deviance isn't about gender). For example, you could write about the different ages males and females peak for offending, then the different crime rates for young men and women, then finish off with **McRobbie & Garber's idea of bedroom culture** (p121).*

9. Assess the New Right explanation of youth deviance. **[24 marks: 8 AO1 + 8 AO2 + 8 AO3]**

This is a full essay question, with equal weight given to knowledge of Sociology, illustration and evaluation.

*You need to make **3 points in favour** of the viewpoint in the question (e.g. that youth subcultures are linked to the Underclass) and **3 opposed** to these New Right views. The best structure is a point-then-criticism, point-then-criticism and point-then-criticism; no conclusion is required (but it might help). For example, you could write about the idea of single parent families not socialising their children properly, then worklessness making young men irresponsible and delinquent, then finish off with **Murray's argument that this underclass is caused by the 'benefits trap' (p129)**. You have 30 minutes for this essay.*

CHAPTER EIGHT – DEVIANCE & THE MEDIA

The Media refers to any type of mass communication, from billboards to those flyers that come through your door offering free pizzas. Here it particularly refers to the news media (newspapers, magazines, TV and radio news, Internet news services) that reports youth deviance.

It's important to remember that the news media is carefully selected (or 'curated'). Most things that happen never get reported: no matter how important they might be for individuals, they're not considered 'news' by the media companies that publish the news. In this case, there are daily incidents of youth deviance (children truant school, two gangs fight, teenagers steal from a shop) that never make the news, though it causes distress to parents, neighbours and shopkeepers.

News is selected in accordance with 'news values.' These include things like **frequency** and **timeliness** (is the incident happening a lot and is it recent?) but also **conflict** and **negativity** (dramatic conflict is interesting and bad news is better than good news) along with **unambiguity** (is it clear who the good guys and bad guys are?).

News values were summed up by American publisher **William Randolph Hearst** in the 1890s: "*If it bleeds, it leads.*" Hearst meant that sensationalist stories of violence and death would always make the front page.

News values influence the way a story is presented: the headline that accompanies it, the choice of wording, the pictures that are used, all chosen to manipulate the audience to respond in a certain way.

Positive Views of the Media

The news media brings us knowledge of what's going on in the world. It educates us about our society, which is far too large and complicated for us to understand it just based on our own social contacts and personal experiences.

More importantly, the news media alerts us to rising threats to our way of life, whether they are crime or political corruption or foreign threats. The news media helps define and sometimes change our shared values. People commonly discuss the news over their tea or coffee breaks. How they react to provocative stories helps set the boundaries of acceptable behaviour; when people come together in shock and outrage, they experience **social solidarity** (a sense of belonging).

The news media also has a role in evolving our shared values. Newspapers run campaigns to reform the law. For example, after a series of knife attacks, the *Daily Express* ran a campaign in 2009 to ban the sale of 'Zombie Knives' (large, stylish weapons based on the knives in video games).

This is a **Functionalist** view of the news. It is based on a **pluralist view of the media**: news companies are driven by profit and deliver the content people want to watch and read; they are not able to control us and instead we the consumers have control over them.

Negative Views of the Media

A different view of the news media is that it distorts our understanding of what is happening in society, promoting fear and outrage. The newspapers in the UK tend to be Right Wing and their campaigns are often to have things banned and to resist the rights of minority groups.

For example, back in 1986 *The Sun* ran a campaign to remove homosexual literature from school libraries, based around a book called *Jenny Lives With Eric & Martin*, supposedly available to children and featuring same-sex parenting. *The Sun* called this a 'direct threat to the nation's children' and the Conservative Government introduced Clause 28 in 1988, banning the 'promotion' of homosexuality in schools (including sex education teaching about homosexuality).

Marxists claim that news stories are curated to support **hegemonic power**, by presenting non-hegemonic groups (e.g. the working classes, ethnic minorities, homosexuals) as threats. The **Marxist instrumentalist view** is that newspapers are owned by 'press barons' who are in league with the ruling classes and manipulate their audiences to be submissive. The **Neo-Marxist view** is that journalists are reasonably independent but still get hired because their views match the owners and editors and don't want to stray too far from the hegemonic line in case they get fired.

Feminists similarly see the news media as promoting patriarchy, with stories that **objectify women** (focusing on their bodies and shaming them for their imperfections) and only showing them in a narrow range of stereotypical roles.

Research: revisit your notes on **1A: Socialisation, Culture & Identity** and combine these ideas with the details about Rupert Murdoch's News Corporation and Clause 28

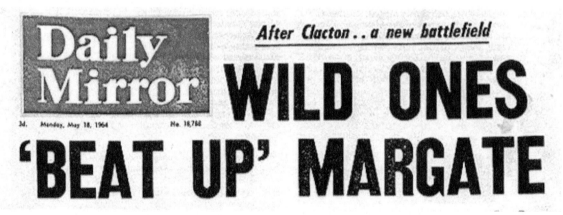

A headline from 1964 about the Seaside Riots (see next page)

AO2 ILLUSTRATION: THE 1964 SEASIDE RIOTS

In 1964, two new Youth Subcultures had emerged in the UK. The Mods were largely working-class but valued a smart and stylish appearance and drove scooters. The Rockers tended to be from more middle-class homes, but preferred a long-haired look, wearing leather jackets and driving motorbikes. The two groups had little to do with each other, following different bands and pursuing different lifestyles.

But in the Easter of 1964, young Londoners descended on the seaside resort of Clacton, enjoying the mobility their motorbikes and scooters offered them. It was a cold and wet day, the youths were bored: fights broke out, with scuffles on the promenade and stone-throwing. There were 64 arrests.

On Easter Monday, the newspapers had headlines like *'Day of Terror by Scooter Groups'* (*Daily Telegraph*) and *'Youngsters Beat Up Town - 97 Leather Jacket Arrests'* (*Daily Express*).

After that reporting, newspaper readers waited anxiously for the next Bank Holiday in May. Thousands of Mods and Rockers descended on Brighton, Clacton, Margate and other resorts, all expecting trouble. The police were there in force. Journalists were there too, taking photographs of the fighting. The headlines reported *'The Battle of Brighton'* (1000 youths involved and 76 arrests). Newspaper editorials predicted the collapse of society, referring to the youths as *'vermin'* and *'mutated locusts wreaking untold havoc on the land'*.

RESEARCH PROFILE: COHEN (1972)

Stan Cohen (1942–2013 and not to be confused with Albert Cohen the Functionalist, p139) wrote a classic in media studies, *Folk Devils & Moral Panics* **(1972)**.

Cohen researched the fights which took place in English seaside resorts on Bank Holidays in 1964 between two youth subcultures: the **Mods** (p120) and the motorbike-riding **Rockers**.

Cohen was an **Interactionist** (p102) influenced by **Becker's Labelling Theory**. He was more interested in the way newspapers reported the events than rather than the events themselves. His study was a mixture of observation, content analysis (looking at the language and images of the 1964 news reports) and interviews.

Cohen concludes that the media reporting was very different from the actual events, but it had a huge influence on the subsequent behaviour of the two sets of youths and the police. In effect, the Media *created* the deviance rather than just reporting it.

Cohen suggested that there are five groups involved in the process of moral panic. There is the **threat** that starts the moral panic, which Cohen calls a "**folk devil**." There are **enforcers of laws**, like the police. There is the **news media** reporting on it and attaching symbolic images to it. There are **politicians**, who sometimes add to the panic. Finally, there is **the public**, which becomes concerned about the threat and demands something be done about it.

DEVIANCE & THE MEDIA: A TOOLKIT

Most of this part of the course draws on **Cohen (1972)** and the ideas in *Folk-Devils & Moral Panics*.

The idea of the Media *causing* deviancy depends on the **Hypodermic Syringe Model** of media influence, which assumes that the Media can 'inject' ideas into its audience and manipulate their behaviour. This in turn assumes that audiences are completely passive, unable to tell truth from fiction and blindly accept what they are told.

Most sociologists reject the Hypodermic Syringe Model as too simplistic. They prefer various **Active Audience Models** that propose that people pick and choose what to pay attention to and what to believe from the Media.

This still leaves a big question about whether a moral panic in the Media really can change the way people think and behave – or whether those changes were about to happen anyway and the Media just happened to be around to report on it. **Cohen's theory** credits the Media with a lot of influence (and Marxist variations on it tend to credit the Media with even more power to control us), but critics point out that a lot of people never read or watch the news and, if they do, they only pay attention to the bits that interest them, like sport. *How many people **really** followed the news reports of the Mods and the Rockers in 1964?*

MORAL PANICS

A **moral panic** is a widespread fear, usually an irrational one, that has been promoted by the news media. It is then fuelled by politicians and often results in new laws or policies that target a group viewed as dangerous. Moral panics often lead to increased social control.

Moral panics often target **marginalised groups** (i.e. subcultures in society or minorities) by drawing on **negative stereotypes**.

*It's worth asking whether a moral panic **always** targets a marginalised group. This would suggest there can never be a moral panic about the behaviour of politicians or celebrities or the middle classes. Is that true?*

Cohen (1972) describes the moral panic over Mods and Rockers in 1964. He describes the five stages of a moral panic:

1. A group is **represented as a threat** to social norms and society at large
2. The news media presents the threat in **simplistic, symbolic ways** that the public can recognise
3. **Public concern** is aroused
4. The authorities (i.e. police, politicians) respond to the threat with **new laws or policies**
5. This leads to **social change** in the community.

Goode & Ben-Yehuda (1994) add more elements of a moral panic, including the idea that it should be **disproportionate** (public concern is greater than the threat deserves) and **volatile** (public interest moves on and the moral panic is forgotten about).

150

AO2 ILLUSTRATION: RECENT MORAL PANICS

Moral panics didn't end in 1964. You have already read about *The Sun* leading a moral panic about homosexuality in schools in 1986 which led to the passage of Clause 28, a classic example of a panic leading to social change. This moral panic coincided with the appearance of the disease AIDS among the homosexual community, so the newspaper focusing on *Jenny Lives With Eric & Martin* was a simplistic, symbolic way of presenting a complicated threat.

After the **9/11 bombing** in 2001, **Islamophobia** became a moral panic, leading to the invasions of Afghanistan and Iraq – the most dramatic sort of new policy and social change imaginable. Images of the burning World Trade Centre towers became a simplistic, symbolic way of presenting the threat.

More recently, moral panics have focused on an **'epidemic' of knife crime** among youth gangs, often linked to single parent families raising 'feral' children and Drill rap music. Photographs of the grisly knives or quotes of Drill lyrics celebrating violence are a simplistic, symbolic way of presenting the threat. This has led to calls to increase the use of police stop & search and stronger sentences for carrying a knife, as well as banning the sale of 'Zombie Knives.'

Research: research more moral panics: crack cocaine, paedophiles, violent video games, the Momo Challenge, football hooligans (especially after Euro 2020), Satanic Ritual Abuse, benefits cheats, illegal immigrants, *Dungeons & Dragons*

FOLK DEVILS

Cohen (1972) argues that when the news media reports on deviant behaviour they construct a narrative with a clear villain: he calls this the **folk devil**. In Cohen's study, the folk devils were the Youth Subcultures of **the Mods and the Rockers**. Creating a folk devil is necessary to start a moral panic.

Cohen claims there are 3 stages to the creation of a folk devil:

1. **Symbolisation:** the folk devil is oversimplified to make them easily recognizable (such as leather-clad Rockers)
2. **Exaggeration:** the facts are distorted (or even invented) to make the threat seem greater (news reporting ignored how small the groups of Mods and Rockers were)
3. **Prediction**: the threat posed by the folk devil is represented to be growing (the reporting after Easter predicted more violence at the May Bank Holiday)

Step 2 (**Exaggeration**) is the controversial part of this theory. Critics point out that some folk devils really are engaged in destructive activities and by drawing our attention to it the news media are performing a public service. For example, the **New Right** (p129) thinks that the **underclass** is a real problem, not a media exaggeration. However, the entire New Right Perspective could be criticised for being one big moral panic.

Cohen is an **Interactionist** and doesn't speculate about why some groups are targeted as folk devils but not others. **Neo-Marxists** like **Stuart Hall (1978**, p131) have an answer to this: they are **non-hegemonic groups** and they serve as a distraction from more serious problems. Hall points out that the British press made a folk devil out of Black Muggers (and by extension, all Black working class people) to cover up an economic crisis in the 1970s.

Functionalists would go further, arguing that society *needs* folk devils to define the boundaries of acceptable behaviour, reinforce (or evolve) **shared values** and promote **social solidarity**. Small groups of people get stigmatised so that this can happen, but that's like having to break eggs to make an omelette. Critics find this view to be disturbingly hard-hearted.

AO2 ILLUSTRATION: RECENT FOLK DEVILS

The moral panic over Islamist terrorism has made Muslims into folk devils, but particularly Muslim women, with campaigns against the face-covering burqa (technically, it's the **niqab**, but 'burqa' seems to have stuck with the public) particularly targeting them. When France banned the wearing of the niqab in public in 2011, **Siobhan Mullally (2011)** suggested that 1900 Muslim women wore it out of a population of 4.7 million French Muslims: 0.04% and that is considered to be an over-estimate. Why such trouble over such a small group? The 'burqa' is a very recognisable image: it oversimplifies a threat in an easily recognisable way.

You have read about *The Sun*'s campaign in the 1980s which made a folk devil out of homosexuals. The story book about a girl with same-sex parents was actually found in a teachers' resource library, not a library used by pupils, but this was not made clear in the reporting. At that time, there was already a lot of fear about homosexuality because of the appearance of AIDS. Homosexuals are a non-hegemonic group (because heteronormativity is mainstream) and AIDS was identified in the 1980s news media as 'the Gay Plague.'

20,000 ARE INFECTED . . . AND IT'S GETTING WORSE

Britain threatened by gay virus plague

DEVIANCY AMPLIFICATION

Cohen (1972) borrows a concept from another Interactionist, **Leslie Wilkins (1964)**, of the **deviancy amplification spiral**. Deviancy amplification is a type of **secondary deviance** (p133) that occurs when **formal agencies of social control** form a big part of the social reaction to deviance – when **labels** are applied by the news media, rather than just your friends and neighbours. Because the news media simplifies and exaggerates, the label it applies is much more negative that the original transgression deserves but also harder to negotiate or remove.

Deviancy amplification becomes a **'spiral'** when police and journalists go looking for more examples of the deviancy. Of course, they find it (or interpret ordinary behaviour as deviant), which adds to the perception that deviancy is increasing and getting out of control. This leads to more arrests and courts passing tougher sentences, which creates the impression of a 'crime wave.'

The **Self-Fulfilling Prophecy (SFP)** means that people accept and internalise the labels the media use. For example, in 1964 Mods and Rockers started genuinely hating each other because of the news media reporting these battles, whereas the first scuffles in Clacton only occurred because the bad weather ruined their holiday and they were bored.

Another ingredient in deviancy amplification is the work of **moral entrepreneurs (Becker, 1963)**. These are people outside of the news media who are pushing for new policies or social change. They are often politicians, but they can also be church groups, celebrities or charities. Moral entrepreneurs 'latch onto' a moral panic and do their best to fuel public concern.

Marxists point out that the deviancy amplification spiral often serves the interests of the ruling class or hegemony and justifies the use of what **Althusser** calls the **Repressive State Apparatus (RSA**, e.g. a police crack-down, p51).

Sometimes moral entrepreneurs will campaign for non-hegemonic groups, such as LGBT groups, ethnic minorities or women. The **2021 murder of Sarah Everard** triggered a moral panic about predatory males and violence against women, with moral entrepreneurs calling for policies like a night-time curfew for men. However, if we use **Goode & Ben-Yehuda's criterion of disproportionality** (p149), then this might *not* be a true moral panic if the threat to women from predatory men is proportionate to the public concern.

AO2 ILLUSTRATION: RECENT MORAL ENTREPRENEURS

One of the most famous moral entrepreneurs in **Mary Whitehouse** (1910-2001). Whitehouse was a teacher and a Christian who was disturbed by changes in British society, especially the sex and violence in the Media. She founded the *Clean Up TV* campaign in 1964 which became the **National Viewers & Listeners Association (NVLA)** in 1965; it became *Mediawatch-UK* in 2001.

Whitehouse campaigned against sex, nudity and violence, swearing and homosexuality in TV, pop music and news reporting. She particularly opposed violence in children's TV and criticised *Doctor Who* for this. She also opposed pornography, especially child pornography.

More recently, moral panics about Islamist terrorism and the 'burqa' have been supported by a moral entrepreneur named **Tommy Robinson**. Robinson co-founded the **English Defence League (EDL)** in 2009 to campaign against the dangers of 'radical Islam.' Robinson has been to prison several times and banned from social media platforms for promoting Hate Speech, but insists he is not against Muslims in general.

RESEARCH PROFILE: FAWBERT (2008)

Jack Fawbert wrote *Hoodies: Folk Devils and a Moral Panic for the New Millennium?* **(2008)** after carrying out a detailed content analysis of newspaper reports about **delinquency** between 2004 and 2008. He found only one article in 2004 that used the word 'hoodie' to describe a delinquent youth.

However, a year later, the **Bluewater Shopping Centre** banned shoppers who wore hoodies and Prime Minister **Tony Blair** promised to clamp down on anti-social behaviour by 'hoodies.' The news media seized on the term 'hoodies' between 2005 and 2007, to describe a deviant Youth Subculture. Fawbert notes that 'Hoodie' would sometimes appear in the headline, but there would be no reference in the story about whether the young criminal was actually wearing one.

This fits the description of a **moral panic**, with a social threat being represented in a simplistic and symbolic way. The Hoodie became a **folk devil**, with facts being exaggerated or even invented. The shopping centre is an example of **social change** as a result. Tony Blair is a **moral entrepreneur** entering the debate and calling for **new policies and punishments**.

Sales of hoodies soared as young people realised they upset people in authority by wearing them. This shows the **deviancy amplification spiral**, as more 'Hoodies' appear.

Banksy's Hoodie With A Knife

EXAM PRACTICE: DEVIANT SUBCULTURES

The OCR exam has three questions in **Paper 1 Section B**. Questions 4-6 are on Families & Relationships and questions 10-12 are on the Media, but this Study Guide is focused on Option 2, which contains questions 7-9:

7. Outline two folk devils in the UK media. **[12 marks: 8 AO1 + 4 AO2]**

This is very similar to Q2 in Section A, but with no source A and B, so it has to come entirely from your own learning. Notice that the importance of AO1 and AO2 is switched: you get more marks for knowledge of Sociology here and far fewer for real life illustrations.

Outline **two** *types of folk devils – probably the Mods/Rockers from 1964 and Hoodies more recently. Each point should have its own paragraph and be supported by evidence from a named sociologist or piece of research. You have 10 minutes to write this*

8. Explain and briefly evaluate the view that deviancy amplification causes deviant behaviour. **[16 marks: 8 AO1 + 4 AO2 + 4 AO3]**

This is very similar to Q2 in Section A, but with no source A and B, so it has to come entirely from your own learning. Notice that the importance of AO1 and AO2 is switched: you get more marks for knowledge of Sociology here and far fewer for real life illustrations.

Make **two sociological points** *about deviancy amplification – perhaps* **secondary deviance** *and* **moral entrepreneurs**. *Each point should have its own paragraph and be supported by evidence from a named sociologist or piece of research. You have 10 minutes to write this.*

9. Assess moral panics as an explanation of youth deviancy. **[24 marks: 8 AO1 + 8 AO2 + 8 AO3]**

This is a full essay question, with equal weight given to knowledge of Sociology, illustration and evaluation.

You need to make **3 points in favour** *of the viewpoint in the question (e.g. that moral panics explain youth deviancy) and* **3 opposed** *to these views. The best structure is a point-then-criticism, point-then-criticism and point-then-criticism; no conclusion is required (but it might help). For example, you could write about the idea of a folk devil being identified as a threat, the media exaggerating and using simplified and symbolic images and the resulting new policies and social change. The differing views of Functionalists, the New Right and Marxists could all come into this as well as the question about whether the moral panic actually causes deviancy. You have 30 minutes for this essay.*

CHAPTER NINE – EVALUATION

In **Paper 1 Section B (Option 2: Youth Subcultures)**, question 8 assesses **AO3**/evaluation and the instruction is to "*briefly evaluate*" while question 9 asks for a developed evaluation.

'Brief evaluation' should be a simple **strength**, **weakness** or **comparison**. A developed evaluation needs to address theoretical or methodological issues. It needs to go deeper than a 'brief evaluation' and look at an issue from alternative perspectives or work through the implications of a viewpoint.

As well as the evaluative points you can find in the preceding chapters, here are some evaluative positions candidates can adopt:

Brief Evaluations

These points are suitable for Q8. You can use them in Q9 as well, but their simplicity makes them hard to turn into developed points, so you might miss out on the higher AO3 band marks. Still, better to write something than nothing at all.

"Not all people…" / Over-generalising

Structuralist Perspectives (like **Functionalism** or traditional **Marxism** and **Feminism**) are particularly prone to sweeping generalisations. They often claim that everyone is motivated by the same thing or experiences the same oppression or wants the same outcomes. For example, Functionalists claim everyone shares the same basic values in society and Feminists claim all women are in some way oppressed.

To evaluate these ideas, point out that not all people fit into this mould. Not all Punks are resisting Capitalism (p140), not all teenage girls socialise in their bedrooms (p121) and not all working class boys are frustrated in school (p139).

If you are writing about some empirical research, point out that its sample group doesn't resemble everyone. Not all delinquent schoolboys are white like the ones that William Chambliss studied (p110).

It's important not to be formulaic. Say *why* not all people are like this: give an example of one of the exceptions. Not all Punks are resisting Capitalism, because some people were only Punks *because they liked the music*. Not all delinquent schoolboys are like Chambliss' schoolboys *because some are Black or Asian and they have their own problems with racism*.

"It's out-of-date..." / Time-locked

You will probably have noticed that an awful lot of sociological research comes from the 1950s, '60s and '70s. Those were important decades when a lot of ground-breaking Sociology was done. But do theories and samples from the 1970s tell us anything about the UK in the 21st century?

To evaluate these studies, point out that so much has changed. **Mass employment in factories** has ended, **equal rights for women** has arrived (at least, in principle), the UK has **become a multicultural society**, the **Internet** has transformed the way we communicate and find out about the world (this last point makes studies from the 1980s and early '90s out-of-date too).

Once again, it's important not to be formulaic. Say **why** one of these changes matters for this particular study: give an example of one of the exceptions. McRobbie & Garber's research into the bedroom culture (p121) is out-of-date *teenagers meet online now and access the Internet from their phones not their bedrooms*. Chambliss' research into the Saints & Roughnecks (p110) is out-of-date *because in the 21st century, schools and towns have CCTV to catch kids truanting or misbehaving*.

"Nature rather than nurture..." / The Nature-Nurture Debate

Sociologists tend to assume that everything is socially constructed, but it's worth remembering that biology might be playing a neglected role in human behaviour.

To evaluate these ideas, point out that a Nativist approach might be better. Rather than explain Youth Culture through social control, maybe there are innate biological changes that go on in Youth.

It would be formulaic just to say "maybe there are innate biological changes" and leave it at that. Say **why** the Nativist approach would be better: give an example of one of the benefits. Take a Nativist approach to studying Youth Culture, *because it might tell you the role testosterone places in youthful aggression in lots of different cultures*.

Developing Evaluations

These points are suitable for Q8 or Q9. Their complexity makes them suitable for turning into developed points, so you can qualify for higher AO3 band marks on Q9.

"It's a macro-perspective / Interactionist critique

Structuralist Perspectives make sweeping generalisations because they study society as a whole and focus on important institutions rather than individual people. The **Interactionist** Perspective criticises this, saying it is better to look at society 'from the bottom up' (a **micro Perspective**). The sociologist Max Weber recommends using *Verstehen* (p68) – empathic understanding – rather than focusing on big trends.

To evaluate these ideas, point out that an Interactionist approach might be better. Rather than studying Punks as a trend in society, take a micro approach and study individual Punks.

As usual, avoid being formulaic. Say *why* the micro approach would be better: give an example of one of the benefits. Take a micro approach to studying Punks, *because they will tell you why they personally are into Punk, which may or may not have anything to do with Capitalism*.

Development

If you bring in Interactionism as the solution to the problem, don't stop there. You could give examples of studies that employ this micro approach (like **Patrick** infiltrating a Glasgow gang, p137) or explain how later research incorporates aspects of the micro approach (like the way Neo-Marxism interviews punks and skinheads).

"This is similar to…" / Comparisons

Sometimes, different sociologists or different Perspectives end up saying similar things, although usually for different reasons Marxists and Feminists both agree there is propaganda and brainwashing (**ideology**) in the news and in schools. Marxists and Functionalists both agree that modern Capitalism is stressful and difficult for ordinary youngsters. Interactionists and Marxists both agree that the police treat young people with suspicion.

To evaluate these ideas, point out the similarity between the sociology you are writing about and another Perspective or research study. If you have explained that Marxists think that the news media is brainwashing, explain that Interactionists also think the news media applies labels.

As usual, don't be formulaic. Say *why* the two approaches are so similar *or* say why they are also different: give an example. Marxists and Interactionist agree on news media because they both think the news doesn't tell us the objective truth, *although Marxists think this comes from serving the ruling class* and *Interactionists focus more on how moral entrepreneurs interfere with the news*.

Development

If you think two Perspectives are similar, don't stop there. You could give examples of studies from each perspective, like **Hall**'s study of moral panics about Black muggers (p131) compared to **Cohen**'s study of Mods & Rockers (p147); or explain how later research incorporates both perspectives, like the Neo-Marxists in the CCCS using Interactionist techniques.

"A Postmodernist would say ..." / Postmodern critique

Postmodernism (p103) makes a powerful criticism of other Perspectives in research from the 1990s or the 21st century.

Postmodernism proposes the big structuralists theories (Functionalism, traditional Marxism and Feminism) are meta-narratives that don't explain anything anymore. Society has become fragmented and fluid and people pick and choose aspects of their Identities. Media saturation has taken place and the difference between media image and reality has broken down.

In order to avoid being formulaic, say *why* a Postmodernist approach would be better: give an example of the benefits. Take a Postmodern approach to studying the Youth Subcultures, *because it will focus on how young people shift fluidly between different styles rather than being loyal to just one subculture.*

Development

If you think Postmodernism is good, don't stop there. You could give examples of studies from the Postmodernist perspective (like **Bennett**'s study of Newcastle clubbers, p124) or explain how Postmodernism incorporates other perspectives (like an awareness of how Capitalism affects people through advertising and branded images which is something Marxists agree with).

"A weakness of this Perspective is ..." / Standard theoretical critiques

Functionalism

Functionalism ignores diversity: Functionalism assumes we are all the same and want the same things, but the things it says we all want tend to be the sort of things that the white middle classes want. Functionalism doesn't take seriously the idea that ethnic minorities, the working class or women might have different goals and values.

Functionalism ignores social injustice: Functionalism assumes that society is harmonious and **meritocratic** but it turns a blind eye to a lot of inequality, corruption and barriers to social mobility. It defends Capitalism as the best system we have discovered for making people healthy and wealthy while ignoring the huge human and environmental cost of Capitalism worldwide. It is also prepared to accept a lot of crime for the sake of consensus.

Functionalism celebrates Western superiority: Functionalists believe in the **'March of Progress'** and claim that the sort of liberal democratic nations you find in Europe, North America and Australia are the most advanced. They think other societies ought to imitate them and immigrants ought to fit in. This ignores many flaws in Western societies (e.g. Capitalism, patriarchy, the 'storm & stress' of Youth which Mead argues doesn't exist in other cultures).

Functionalism overrates the biological: Functionalists believe society reflects unchangeable biological needs or 'human nature.' Critics argue there is no such thing as 'human nature' and that everything is **socially constructed**. 'Human nature' is often used to excuse youth deviance due to 'storm & stress' and the need to vent frustration.

Marxism

Marxism ignores progress: In the last 200 years, Capitalist societies have abolished slavery, set up human rights, created a welfare state and free education and healthcare for all. Marxists often talk as if this hasn't happened or as if it happened *in spite of* Capitalism. This pessimistic view of the past and the future perhaps exaggerates social injustice as much as Functionalism downplays it.

Marxism is a conspiracy theory: It's standard for Marxists to argue that the Media (especially the news), Education and the Workplace are all controlled by a sinister group of billionaires who brainwash everyone through **ideology**. This underestimates the independence of many journalists, teachers and bosses as well as the ability of ordinary people to think for themselves and work out what's true.

Marxists assume class is homogenous: *Homogenous* means 'all the same' and traditional Marxists think that all working class people share the same relationship to labour and power. However, **Neo-Marxists** (p131) are more aware of **intersecting Identities** and how behaviour is shaped by the particular circumstances.

Marxism offers no solutions: You don't have to be a Marxist to spot the Capitalism has flaws – Functionalists would admit *that*! Marxists argue that Capitalism is intrinsically rotten and destructive, and it needs to be replaced rather than reformed. But replaced with what? Marxism can be accused of criticising Capitalism without offering a coherent alternative. Similarly, it identifies Youth Deviance as resistance, but doesn't suggest what can be done about it's destructive aspects.

Feminism

Feminism ignores biology: Feminists insist that gender is **socially constructed,** and it certainly is up to a point. However, Psychology reveals lots of biological differences in brain structure, hormones and genes between the sexes and it's unlikely that *none* of this makes *any* difference to social behaviour. But if Gender Identity is even partly based on unchangeable sexual differences, then some of the situations women are in might not be *entirely* due to Patriarchy.

Feminism ignores progress: In the last century women have won the vote, the right to be educated at university and manage their own affairs. In Britain, the Sexual Discrimination Act (1975) has outlawed sexual discrimination. Feminism can be accused of downplaying this progress and exaggerating the scale of injustice. However, the Sarah Everard murder can be used to show that women in the 21st century are still not safe.

Feminists assume gender is homogenous: As with Marxists and social class, traditional Feminists are accused of treating all women as if they experienced the same oppression – which in practice means assuming that the difficulties of White women are typical for all women. Clearly, young women (and especially young lesbian women) have different experiences.

Feminists ignore the oppression of men: Feminists sometimes seem to assume that Masculinity is homogenous, and all men are complicit in the Patriarchy, but men are much more likely than women to die by violence, to be victims of crime and to work in dangerous conditions. Many young men are also victims of oppression and die in dangerous jobs, through violence or suicide.

Interactionism

Interactionism cannot be generalised: Because it tends to do research on small groups, studying micro relationships and beliefs, it's hard to generalise the conclusions of Interactionism to other groups or society on a macro level.

Interactionists cannot be objective: The close-up and personal nature of Interactionist research and its focus on *Verstehen* makes it very **subjective** – just a matter of opinion – whereas Sociology claims to be a social *science* that explores facts in an **objective** way.

Interactionism is an incomplete explanation: Even when Interaction identifies processes that seem to be quite generalisable – like the **Self-Fulfilling Prophecy** – its small-scale micro view means it doesn't explore where these processes come from. Marxists argue that Interactionism is incomplete as an explanation without including Capitalism and **ruling class ideology**. Functionalists would also say Interactionism needs to explain how the experiences of little groups fit into a theory of society's functions and requirements.

Postmodernism

Postmodernism ignores continuing modernity: The Internet has made huge changes to our lives, along with technology like mobile phones and satellite TV. However, life for many people continues as it did in the 1960s, '70s and '80s: they live in nuclear families, work in factories or offices, take part in religious worship and live in social classes. Only a minority of people – and perhaps, only in a few big cities – enjoys the unusual, ever-changing, online lifestyles that Postmodernism claims are typical. This is Giddens' argument for **Late Modernity** (p104).

Postmodernists reject objective truth: By rejecting **meta-narratives**, Postmodernism rejects objective truth. Nothing is absolutely and provably true, it can only ever be subjective truth (true-for-you or true-as-you-see-it). But how can social problems be solved unless we agree they objectively *are* problems? Why should sociological research be taken seriously if it's only a point of view? How can we tell good points of view from wild conspiracy theories and 'fake news'?

Postmodernism only applies to some topics: Postmodernism is great for explaining shifts in style and fashion, personal Identity, consumer choice and lifestyles, especially online lifestyles. It's less good for tackling the harder topics of poverty, discrimination and violence. It **also lacks political solutions** for tackling these things. Marxism tends to inspire Left Wing (Labour) policies and Functionalism (and sometimes the New Right) inspires Right Wing (Conservative) policies, but it's difficult to see any policies that have come from Postmodernism.

The New Right

The New Right lacks empirical support: Most of the support for the New Right comes from news stories about working class deviance – but those stories might be exaggerated. Hard evidence for the existence of an **underclass** is not plentiful and there's even less evidence for a whole group of people (rather than a few individuals) who reject society's values, don't want to work, don't want to live in families and embrace crime as a lifestyle.

The New Right demonises the vulnerable: The New Right is accused of 'punching down' – targeting the group in society that most needs help and making them out to be monstrous and calling for any sort of help (in the form of benefits) to be taken away. **Marxists** find it fairly easy to characterise the New Right as a **hegemonic attack on the poor**. However, Marxists can be characterised as glamorising delinquents and criminals as noble underdogs and ignoring the damage they do in society.

The New Right exaggerates deviancy: The New Right presents the underclass as a growing problem that threatens the whole of society. Even **Functionalists** criticise this approach as alarmist. Functionalist believe that deviancy is necessary and ultimately benefits society. However, the New Right emerged partly because both Functionalists and Marxists seemed to be making excuses for crime rather than doing anything practical to put a stop to it.

Development

If you offer a theoretical weakness, don't stop there. You could give examples of studies that illustrate that weakness (like Murray's warning that single mothers are raising feral boys and promiscuous girls illustrates the New Right demonising the vulnerable). Alternatively, follow through the implications of this weakness (what would happen if politicians acted on Murray's suggestions) or bring in other Perspectives that have something to say about this weakness (like Marxists characterising the attack as serving hegemonic power).

EXAM PRACTICE: SECTION B

The OCR exam has three questions in **Paper 1 Section B**. Questions 4-6 are on Families & Relationships and questions 10-12 are on the Media, but this Study Guide is focused on Option 2, which contains questions 7-9:

7. Outline two moral panics in the UK media. **[12 marks: 8 AO1 + 4 AO2]**

This is very similar to Q2 in Section A, but with no source A and B; you get more marks for knowledge of Sociology here and far fewer for real life illustrations.

*Choose **two** moral panics to outline – probably the Mods/Rockers from 1964 and Hoodies more recently. It's a good idea to refer to named sociologists (like Cohen and Fawbert) and you should definitely use some sociological terminology (like moral panics, symbolisation, non-hegemonic groups). Then offer examples and make sure each example has an explanation of **why** it is a moral panic. For example, "Mods & Rockers had a brief skirmish in Clacton but the newspapers exaggerated it into 'Day of Terror!'"*

8. Explain and briefly evaluate the view that youth deviance is related to social class. **[16 marks: 8 AO1 + 4 AO2 + 4 AO3]**

This is similar to Q3 in Section A, but again with fewer marks given to AO2 illustration.

*Write three paragraphs: **two argue in favour** of the question and the **third paragraph argues against** (e.g. that youth deviance is not related to being working class). For example, you could write about trends in working class deviance, Marxist views on working class youth deviance and Chambliss' study of the **Saints & the Roughnecks (p110)**.*

9. Assess postmodern explanations of youth subcultures. **[24 marks: 8 AO1 + 8 AO2 + 8 AO3]**

This is a full essay question, with equal weight given to knowledge of Sociology, illustration and evaluation.

*You need to make **3 points in favour** of the viewpoint in the question (e.g. that youth subcultures are fluid now) and **3 opposed** to these postmodern views. The best structure is a point-then-criticism, point-then-criticism and point-then-criticism; no conclusion is required (but it might help). For example, you could write about the **Postmodernist** idea of fluidity using Makina as an example, then Bennet's argument for **Maffesoli's theory of Neo-Tribes (p104)** and **Postman's theory of the disappearance of childhood (p83)**. You have 30 minutes for this essay.*

KEY RESEARCH

The 20 studies here cover all the topics that arise in **2B: Youth Subcultures Option** and they will prove just as useful in later sections too. Start learning them. For each study, I include the key terms, a Perspective (if relevant) and the particular topics it is linked to.

Cashmore (1997): *The Black Culture Industry*, hybridity, Hip-Hop as a commodity; **Postmodernism**; youth subculture & ethnicity, p122

CCCS (1970s): *Resistance Through Rituals* etc.; **Neo-Marxism**; subcultures & class, deviant spectacular subcultures, p113

Chambliss (1973): *The Saints & the Roughnecks*, labelling; **Interactionism, Neo-Marxism**; youth culture, subcultures & class, deviant delinquent subcultures, p110

Clarke, Cohen (1976): *Resistance Through Rituals*, skinheads, symbolic resistance; **Neo-Marxism**; youth subcultures & class, deviant spectacular subcultures, p119

Cloward & Ohlin (1960): legitimate & illegitimate opportunity structures, criminal, conflict, retreatist; **Functionalism**; deviant criminal/gang subcultures, p136

Cohen, A (1955): *Delinquent Boys*, status frustration; **Functionalism**; deviant delinquent/anti-school subcultures, p139

Cohen, S (1972): *Folk Devils & Moral Panics*, 1964 Mods v Rockers riots; **Interactionism**; media & deviance, p147

Durkheim (1895): society of saints; **Functionalism**; youth deviance, p128

Eisenstadt (1956): *Generation To Generation*, anomie, social integration, transgression; **Functionalism**; youth culture, youth deviance, p108

Fawbert (2008): *Hoodies: Folk Devils for the New Millennium?* Moral panic over hoodies; **Interactionist**; media & deviance, p152

Hall (1978): *Policing the Crisis*, moral panic over Black muggers; **Neo-Marxism**; subculture & ethnicity, deviant delinquent subcultures, media & deviance, p131

Hebdige (1979): *Subculture: The Meaning of Style*, punks, resistance, bricolage, incorporation; **Neo-Marxism**; deviant spectacular subcultures, p140

Jefferson (1976): *Resistance Through Rituals*, Teddy Boys; **Neo-Marxism**; deviant delinquent/spectacular subcultures, p135

Mac An Ghaill (1988): *Young, Gifted & Black*, ethnicity, gender and youth deviance; **Marxism**; youth deviance, p144

Maffesoli (1977): *The Time of the Tribes*, neo-tribes replace subcultures; Postmodernism; youth subcultures & hybridity, p124

Mead (1928): *Coming of Age in Samoa*; youth culture without Storm & Stress, p99

McRobbie & Garber (1976): *Resistance Through Rituals*, invisibility of girls, bedroom culture; **Feminism**; youth subcultures & gender, p121

Miller (1958): working class focal concerns; **Functionalism**; subcultures & class, deviant delinquent/anti-school subcultures, p130

Murray (1984): underclass; **New Right**; subcultures & class, deviant delinquent/gang subcultures, p129

Patrick (1973): *A Glasgow Gang Observed*, participant observation; **Interactionist**; deviant gang subcultures, p137

Patterns & Trends

You also need to be able to cite some patterns and trends in youth deviance (p141):

Joseph Rowntree Foundation: 4/10 males and 1/10 females cautioned or arrested at some point; only 5% responsible for 50% of crime

Mayor of London's Office (2019): 75% of offending in top 10 most deprived areas of London

Ministry of Justice (2019): children cautioned or sentenced has fallen 83% in last 10 years; 85% are boys, 15% girls; 69% are White, 16% Black, 6% Asian (out of 84%, 5%, 9% of population)

National Prison Survey (2020): 41% of convicts from manual classes

Prison Reform Trust (2010): survey of 200 young offenders found 50% from deprived backgrounds, 75% with absent fathers; also school exclusion

Youth Justice Board (2009): peak age for female offending is 15 but 18 for males

FURTHER RESEARCH

These studies are less central to any argument. Some of them just reference a useful piece of terminology. Others offer criticism of a Key Study or are the original research that a Key Study is criticising.

Adler (1975): Liberation Thesis, p133

Althusser (1970): RSA and ISA, p51

Baudrillard (1970): hyper-reality, p104

Becker (1963): *Outsiders*, labelling theory, p103

Bennett (1999): supports Maffesoli, p124

Brake (1980): subcultures as magical solutions, p132

Campbell et al. (2000): differences between males & female youth deviance, p143

Cohen (1955): status frustration, p139

Davies (1967): deviance is a safety valve, p128

Faludi (1999): *Stiffed*, delinquents obsessed with celebrity, p75

Giddens (1999): *Runaway World*, Late Modernity, p104

Goode & Ben-Yehuda (1994): adds elements to moral panics, p149

Greer (2014): critiques *Everyday Sexism Project*, p107

Hodkinson (2002): why Goths continue into adulthood, p127

Hollands & Chatterton (2002): youth culture is commercialised now, p123

Johal (1998): Brasians, hyper-ethnic style, p121

Lemert (1967): secondary deviance, p133

Lyotard (1979): end of meta-narratives, p104

Matza (1964): Drift Theory, subterranean values, p133

Polhemus (1997): the 'Supermarket of Style,' p116

Postman (1994): *The Disappearance of Childhood*; breakdown of youth, p104

Sewell (1997): Black subculture of hyper-masculinity, criticises Mac An Ghaill (1988), p144

St Croix (2017): criticises NCS, p109

Freeman (1983): criticises Mead (1928) p99

Gramsci (--): introduces idea of hegemonic control to **Neo-Marxism**, 131

Hall, G S (1904): coined *'Sturm und Drang'* (Storm & Stress), p97

Rimmer (2010): studied Makina fans, p123

Smith et al. (2005): working class youths have adversarial relationship with police, p141

Willis (1977): *Learning To Labour*, criticises Cohen's status frustration, p41

Willis (1990): end of spectacular youth subcultures, p123

Young (1984): bulimic society, p42

GLOSSARY

Alienation: Marxist idea similar to **anomie** that workers under Capitalism become alienated from their labour and themselves by dehumanising conditions

Anomie: literally means "without norms" and it refers to the sense of disconnection and anxiety that occurs when people do not feel a connection to their society and their work; Functionalists say it is caused by the breakdown of **social solidarity** and a lack of **value consensus**

Bedroom Culture: according to **McRobbie & Garber (1976**, p121), the way teenage girls resist hegemonic and patriarchal culture in private spaces, through the consumption of media products (e.g. teen magazines, pop music) and experimenting with appearance

Capitalism: an economic system that promotes the private ownership of property, the pursuit of profit and the concentration of wealth in the hands of a minority of people; the opposite is Communism, which abolishes private property to make everyone economically equal

CCS: Centre for Contemporary Cultural Studies at the University of Birmingham; carried out research into **Spectacular Youth Subcultures** from a **Neo-Marxist** Perspective

Cultural Capital: an understanding of high culture that gives you access to the privileges of the wealthy elite, according to **Bourdieu (1984**, p19**)**

Culture: the set of norms and values passed on by one generation to the next, including a version of history and traditional institutions that make up a way of life; cultures vary from one society to another and change (slowly) over time

Deviance: Behaviour that goes against **norms** and **values**

Feminism: a sociological Perspective that identified conflict between the sexes; believes in a Patriarchy which subordinates women and maintains male power through coercion and violence

Folk Devil: a group identified as a threat to society during a **moral panic**

Functionalism: a sociological Perspective that promotes consensus around shared values; believes in a biological basis for human social behaviour and the inevitability of deviance

Gender: the norms and values linked to biological sex; males are often expected to behave in a masculine way and females in a feminine way: male/female are sexes but masculine/feminine are genders

Gender role: the social expectations that go with gender; masculinity is often linked with aggression, ambition, intelligence and high status; femininity is often linked with passivity, emotion and subordinate status; gender roles lead to the expectation of different career choices for men and women and different expectations about responsibilities in the home

Globalisation: a process going on that makes different parts of the world more interconnected through travel, global **Capitalism** and the **Mass Media**

Habitus: your lifestyle and attitudes (including things like dress, accent and values) which place you in a particular social class, according to **Bourdieu (1984, p19)**

Hegemony: the dominance of one group and their culture in society; hegemonic culture is the version of culture that commands the most respect; according to **Neo-Marxists** hegemonic culture manufactures consent

Ideology: a set of ideas and values that influence how people interpret society; ideology is usually promoted by the **hegemonic** culture hides and justifies things which go against that culture; for example, a racist ideology might make people ignore racism or (if they can't ignore it) view racism as justified

Interactionism: a sociological Perspective that adopts a micro (small scale) approach; believes in understand individual motives and perceptions, often through examining how people play social roles or internalise **labels**

Intersectional: A 21st century approach to Sociology which focuses on how different identities combine to create privilege or oppression

Labelling Theory: an **Interactionist** explanation of deviance due to social labels with master status that are internalised, producing a self-fulfilling prophecy, according to **Becker (1963)**

Latent function: The hidden effects of social institutions, that befit society without us noticing

Manifest function: The obvious effects of social institutions, that benefit society in ways we all recognise

Marxism: a sociological Perspective that identifies conflict between social classes; believes in a **ruling class** exploiting a **working class**, both through violet force and **ruling class ideology**

Mass Media: technological forms of communication that can reach millions (or billions of people); traditionally radio, TV, film and print but now including the digital media, such as websites, social media, text messaging and mobile phones

Meritocracy: A system that rewards talent and effort with social advancement; specifically, the idea that education recognises and gives qualifications to the most intelligent people, assigning them to the most important jobs with the biggest rewards. The opposite is **social reproduction**.

Meta-Narrative: a 'Big Story' or grand philosophy that offers an explanation for everything (e.g. Christianity, Marxism, science, democracy) which is impossible to accept for **Postmodernists**

Moral Panic: process where the Media identifies a group as a threat, exaggerates its importance, arouses public concern and brings about new policies and social change

Multiculturalism: the idea that society can and should include people from different cultures without demanding that they abandon their native culture in order to assimilate; may be conceived as a 'melting pot' of hybridised cultures or a 'salad bowl' of distinct cultures respecting each other's differences

Neo-Marxism: several new interpretations of **Marxism** that emerged in the 1970s and became mainstream in the 1990s, incorporating elements of **Interactionism** to Marxist thought

New Right: a sociological Perspective that proposes we are experience social collapse brought on by a welfare culture that rewards worklessness and deviance in the **Underclass**

Norms: ways of behaving seen as acceptable or expected in society; based on underlying **values**

Patriarchy: The way society is structured around the interests of males, giving status to masculine behaviour and values and systematically subordinating women; masculine **hegemony** in society

Postmodernism: a sociological Perspective that proposes we are living in a new phase of social development, characterised by media saturation, diversity, choice, fluidity and fragmentation

Privilege: the advantages a person has, perhaps without realising it, because they belong to high-status groups or have Identities that are respected in society

Ruling class: A **hegemonic** group in society that controls the wealth and power, supported by an ideology that either hides or justifies their influence; Marx termed the ruling class 'the bourgeoisie.'

Ruling class ideology: a set of beliefs promoted by the ruling class to preserve their power over the working class; ideology hides the injustice in society and justifies it when it cannot hide it

Semiology: technique for interpreting symbolic or coded behaviour to reveal its sociological meaning, popular with **Neo-Marxists**

Social class: A system for separating people based on their economic position (wealth, income, status); originally a split between the **ruling class** and **working class**, but later admitting of a middle class in between and now many more classes

Socialisation: The process of acquiring norms and values due to upbringing (primary socialisation) and education/experience (secondary socialisation)

Social reproduction: the opposite of **Meritocracy**; the idea that social divisions are reproduced each generation despite the education people receive

Social solidarity: The experience of 'belonging' in society, linked to **value consensus**; it is the opposite of **anomie**

Spectacular Youth Subculture: several very visible and socially shocking youth subcultures that appeared in the 1950s, '60s and '70s; studied by the **CCS**

Subculture: a group within society that shares some of the **norms and values** of mainstream society but also has distinctive norms and values of its own

Transgression: Behaviour that goes against the rules or laws; similar to **deviance**

Underclass: term used by the **New Right** for a class below the working class, characterised by single mothers on benefits, poorly socialised children and irresponsible, workless and crime-prone adult males

Value consensus: The set of norms and values around which there is (supposedly) broad agreement in society; includes views on history, religion, morality, lifestyle and wealth

Values: powerful ideas shared by people in a culture about what is right and desirable and what is shameful or wrong; often expressed in behaviour as **norms**

Verstehen: A term used by **Max Weber** (p68) to mean 'empathic understanding' rather than studying social behaviour in a purely detached and scientific way

Western culture: the culture of the UK, European countries, North America and Australia, that emerged out of the shared experience of Christianity, the Industrial Revolution and the development of democracy; an important part of **Global Culture**; responsible for developing Capitalism

White collar crime: crime carried out by powerful people in the course of doing their respectable jobs; includes embezzling money, tax fraud, breaking health & safety regulations and environmental pollution.

Working class: The majority group in society that is systematically excluded from access to wealth and power; controlled by **ideology** and the threat of force by the **ruling class**; Marx terms the working class 'the proletariat.'

ABOUT THE AUTHOR

Jonathan Rowe is a teacher of Religious Studies, Psychology and Sociology at Spalding Grammar School and he creates and maintains **www.psychologywizard.net** and the **www.philosophydungeon.weebly.com** site for Edexcel A-Level Religious Studies. He has worked as an examiner for various Exam Boards but is not affiliated with OCR. This series of books grew out of the resources he created for his students. Jonathan also writes novels and creates resources for his hobby of fantasy wargaming. He likes warm beer and smooth jazz.

Jonathan has created the **Sociology Robot** YouTube channel with video lectures supporting the material in this Study Guide.

Printed in Great Britain
by Amazon